BARBAROSSA

IN ITALY

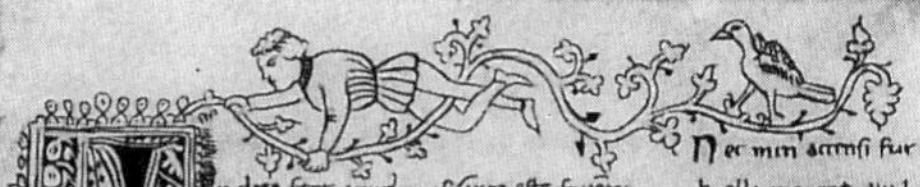

BARBAROSSA

IN ITALY

EDITED AND
TRANSLATED BY
THOMAS CARSON

ITALICA PRESS
NEW YORK
1994

ITALICA PRESS, INC.
595 Main Street
New York, New York 10044

Library of Congress Cataloging-in-Publication Data
Carmen de gestis Frederici I imperatoris in Lombardia. English.
  Barbarosa in Italy / edited and translated by Thomas Carson.
      p. cm.
  Includes bibliographical references (p.).
  ISBN 0-934977-30-5 : $14.50
  1. Frederick I, Holy Roman Emperor, ca. 1123-1190. 2. Lombardy
(Italy)–History–To 1535. 3. Milan (Italy)–History–To 1535.
4. Holy Roman Empire–History–Frederick I, 1152-1190.   I. Carson,
Thomas, 1940- . II. Title.
DD149.C364 1994
943'.025'092–dc20   94-27071
                                                             CIP

Printed in the United States of America
5 4 3 2 1

This book is dedicated to the
blessed memory of Aunt Helen.

.

BARBAROSSA'S
ITALY

25   50 Miles

CONTENTS

ILLUSTRATIONS

PREFACE

When I began this project, I had hoped only to bring before the English-speaking public a fine example of an undeservedly neglected art form, the Latin historical epic of medieval Italy. But as I examined the literature on the subject, I realized that its scholars were not always reading each other, and merely by synthesizing this material I could provide a useful service to those interested in medieval studies.

This literature is not vast, but since the poem has no established title, and since it was written by an anonymous author, *Barbarossa in Italy* poses for the bibliographer a severe test, which is made more complex because the poem belongs equally to two disciplines, history and literature.

Also the work is part of the heritage of two nations, Italy and Germany. When *Barbarossa in Italy* was discovered over one hundred and ten years ago, the international cooperation displayed in the attempt to identify and to evaluate it was laudable. But since then, there have been times when scholars from both countries seem to have labored in ignorance of each other's efforts. Yet both nations have made important contributions. In fact the history of its scholarship, tied as it is to the times that produced it, is almost as fascinating as the poem itself.

The English-speaking world has shown little interest in the poem. Only two English scholars have commented on it, and one of them, S. T. Collins, wrote in Latin for an Italian journal. Few Americans have written on the subject.

This neglect is to our loss, for it is a valuable historical document and an excellent piece of literature.

In the presentation that follows, I have tried to carry the discussion forward in a number of areas, as well as to summarize important theories that were developed about the poem in the past. It is my hope that my introduction will provoke further investigation of this admirable work and the problems that surround it.

Many people deserve special thanks for their help in producing this book. I am grateful to Frank O. Copley for his encouragement early in the process and his suggestion that the poem should be translated line for line in iambic pentameter. Robert Houbeck was very helpful to me in obtaining some of the material that was difficult to find. Stephan Tonsor, James Walz, and Larry Trudeau are in my debt for their careful reading of the manuscript. I would also like to thank Ronald G. Musto and Eileen Gardiner for all their work in bringing the manuscript to print. I must also mention the graciousness with which I was treated by Rev. Leonard Boyle O.P. and the staff of the Vatican Library as well as by those at the American Academy in Rome and the Biblioteca Nazionale Centrale Vittorio Emanuele II, and the Biblioteca Civica A. Mai in Bergamo. Special thanks are due to my wife Dorothy and my parents for their understanding.

INTRODUCTION

With this translation I place before the English-reading public a fine example of the Latin historical epic of medieval Italy, an undeservedly neglected form of literature that attempted to enhance the narration of contemporary history by recounting it in verse that was based on classical models. Although numerous poems of this genre were produced, *Barbarossa in Italy* is the first to be translated into English. Its author, who probably wrote in the 1160s, is unknown, but he was a gifted poet and a remarkable storyteller, who was nourished by the classical revival of the twelfth century. He tells of the events that he found relevant to Emperor Frederick Barbarossa's first two Italian campaigns, which took place between 1154 and 1162; and the work is not complete because it ends abruptly in the midst of the battle of Carcano in 1160.

The untitled manuscript was found in the Vatican Library in 1877 by Ernesto Monaci, a young professor at the University of Rome; and the problems surrounding the work that confronted him over a hundred years ago are with us today. What should the poem be called, and why is it incomplete? Who was the poet, and when did he write? What were his sources, and what is the epic's historical value? What is its literary worth? The following introduction attempts to respond to these questions, and if it does not solve them definitively, it can at least make the reader aware of the fascinating scholarship that they generated in Italy and Germany, the countries where the poem has found the most interest. It

XI

has received little attention in either the United States or the British Commonwealth.

I. THE BACKGROUND

The Italy in which Barbarossa found himself and the Germany from which he came were very different from the modern nations that they are today, and so some discussion of the medieval world is necessary for a modern reader to appreciate fully the circumstances that influenced the poem and its protagonists. This section attempts to provide that background, although in no way does it pretend to be a comprehensive treatment of the medieval period or of Frederick's reign.[1]

Frederick I, who was nicknamed Red Beard (*Barbarossa* in Italian), ruled from 1152 to 1190, and considered himself a Roman emperor, a descendant of the ancient Caesars, but in truth his empire is more accurately traced only to 962, when a German king, Otto I (936-73), was crowned by the pope. Otto was no dreamer yearning to recapture ancient glory, but a pragmatic ruler born into a beleaguered society. He saw the imperial title as a means of enhancing his power, both in Italy, where the prestige of the empire might allow him some control, and in Germany, where an honor bestowed by the papacy might augment his authority, since Otto used the clergy there to exercise his will. It was then in his interest to have good relations with the pope by assuming the role of defender of the Church in exchange for the imperial title. In his eyes the pope became a dependent, and in the course of events, he deposed the man who crowned him.

In general Otto's successors followed his policy for the next hundred years, but the control that he had exercised was severely compromised by the Investiture Conflict, a great struggle that took place between the popes and emperors in the eleventh and twelfth centuries. It was a crisis over the relationship between lay and clerical authority, and it takes its name from the ceremony of investiture, the act of establishing or ratifying a person in his office by giving him the symbols of authority. Ostensibly the conflict involved the question of whether the laity had the right to appoint and invest the clergy, and this struck at the heart of the political system.

Although the struggle seemed to end in 1122 in a compromise agreement called the Concordat of Worms, in the opinion of many scholars, the conflict had almost fatal consequences for imperial authority. For twenty-six years one of Otto's successors, Henry IV (1056-1106), was excommunicated (i.e., he was no longer considered part of the Christian community) with dire consequences for imperial prestige. Also while pope and emperor were at each other's throat, the German nobility and the Italian cities were able to increase their independence. In addition, the extinction of the Salian dynasty with the death of Emperor Henry V in 1125 exacerbated factional strife that was already in progress. One of these contending parties was named after the Welf family (later called *Guelph* in Italian), which often looked to the papacy for support. The imperial party took its name from the castle Weibling, which belonged to its leading family, the Hohenstaufen. In Italy they were known eventually as the *Ghibellines*. In the period extending from 1125 to Barbarossa's assumption of power in 1152, there were two emperors, a Guelph, Lothar of Supplinburg, and a Ghibelline,

Conrad III, neither of whom could end the internecine struggle.

Against this background of religious conflict and civil war, the achievement of Frederick Barbarossa, who is considered by many to be the greatest of the medieval emperors, is remarkable in spite of its limited scope. His accession to the throne was a compromise, since his father was a Hohenstaufen, Frederick the One-eyed, the duke of Swabia, and his mother Judith was a Welf. Frederick's greatest strength lay in his ability to assess realistically his circumstances and exploit his opportunities to the fullest. For example, he realized that there was no effective way to break the power that the princes had won during the Investiture Conflict. But by granting legal recognition to their gains, he could make them his vassals and receive the feudal dues that were owed him. And it cost him nothing. In spite of this, since the magnates still held much (allodal) land for which there was no obligation, and since Frederick had no feudal authority over the lesser vassals who were subordinated directly to the princes, his control was never as strong as that which the English and French kings exerted.

Barbarossa also showed great skill in the way he handled his chief rival, Henry the Lion, but again he did not achieve all he would have liked. At first he insured peace in Germany by supporting Henry's claim to the duchies of Bavaria and Saxony, but when Frederick felt betrayed by Henry's refusal to go on an Italian campaign with him, he sided with Henry's enemies and was able to use the legal system to confiscate his duchies. Yet he was not able to keep the land under his direct control, but had to give it out again to other men.

Introduction

Perhaps if Frederick had been able to restrict his activity to Germany, his reign might have been an unqualified success; but Italy beckoned, and it was a very different place. It was an area of independent city-states that were undergoing a political revolution. The urban populace, which itself was divided by class and family loyalties, was asserting authority over lay lords and bishops by forming autonomous city governments called "communes." The name came to signify the citizens or their common assembly that met ostensibly to decide matters of importance, although most often the real power was in the hands of smaller councils, often composed of the wealthier elements of the city, that could work more efficiently. In fact, the chief authority was a small group of elected officials called "consuls," a title taken from the ancient Roman Republic, and symbolic of the communes' fierce sense of independence.

The rise of communal government could have violent consequences. For example, Gregory, bishop of Bergamo, was murdered in 1146, probably as a result of such a power struggle. In addition, communes expanded their authority over adjacent rural areas by subjugating villages and the neighboring feudal classes. Since the drive for domination did not stop at the borders, the stronger cities continued to grow at the expense of neighboring towns, which, like Lodi and Como in the poem (vv. 17-20), at times faced complete destruction. These local problems were central to those involved in them, but the tensions they produced were often masked under an allegiance to the larger causes of Guelph and Ghibelline. For instance, Bergamo, having two cathedrals, had two cathedral chapters, which were continually at odds over matters of local concern. But one, S. Vincenzo, was considered pro-papal, and the other, S. Alessandro, pro-imperial. Their loyalty was elastic, however, since both chapters would take help from either pope or emperor when it was in their interest to do so.

The northern cities also participated in a general European cultural revival, often inspired by ancient Latin literature, which Charles Homer Haskins called "the Renaissance of the twelfth century." By medieval standards education was widespread. For example, Milan had four well-known schools and many others besides, including probably a law school. Bologna is the home of the first university in the West to attain a legal personality. There was an abundance of educated men, some of whom spoke Greek as well as Latin, and there was even an Arabist, Gerard of Cremona, who has had the translation of over ninety works attributed to him.

It is through the eyes of one of these educated men that we will follow Frederick on the first two of his six expeditions to Italy, where he spent sixteen of his thirty-eight years in power. His reasons for devoting so much time there are numerous and complex. First, like the poet of this poem, Frederick was enamored of the classical tradition. He saw himself as heir to ancient Rome and spoke openly of Constantine, Theodosius, and Justinian as his predecessors. He also had some of his legislation placed in Justinian's great compilation of Roman law, the *Corpus Iuris Civilis*. So Italy, filled with reminiscences of the ancient empire, necessarily had an important role in his thinking. He certainly had a right to this territory, because in addition to the imperial dignity, he was entitled to the iron crown of Lombardy, an Italian kingdom that included most of north-central Italy with the exception of Venice. When in the poem Frederick crossed the Alps (vv. 77-80, 2597-2603), he went to a plain called Roncaglia, where according to custom he held a general assembly or diet of the Italian kingdom. There the great vassals of the realm and the representatives of the city-states came to take oaths of loyalty, and the king heard complaints and held court.

But there were other, tangible, reasons to direct his interest south. Northern Italy belonged to a central grouping of lands that included Burgundy and Switzerland, which Frederick wanted to use as a base for a territorial state. Also, the cities of northern Italy were the beneficiaries of the increase in trade and population that had taken place in the last several hundred years, and the revenue they could produce for Frederick was greater than the total income of either French or English king. To control that area was to make himself the richest sovereign in Europe.

In addition to the rich Lombard cities, Italy was also the seat of the papacy, and it was in Frederick's interest to remain on good terms with Rome or to try to control it with puppets. He also had to take cognizance of the thriving Norman kingdom in Sicily and southern Italy. Having wrested Sicily from Moslem control in the eleventh century, these Normans were legally vassals of the pope, but really they were an independent force that was a matter of concern for both the papacy and the empire. Several times Frederick had made plans to conquer them, and although he never attained his goal, he was able to marry his son to the eventual heir of that kingdom. The Italian situation was further complicated by a strong Byzantine interest.

Therefore Frederick's Italian campaigns were undertaken for a variety of reasons, most of which our poet does not discuss in his account that covers just the first two expeditions. The first began in 1154 and was a coronation trip, for which preparation had been made the year before with the Treaty of Constance. By this agreement, Pope Eugenius III consented to crown Frederick and to place ecclesiastical sanctions against his enemies. In return the emperor would suppress the communal movement in Rome (which desired urban independence as much as any of its northern counterparts), make no peace with the Normans, and grant no land in Italy to the Byzantine Greeks. In addition to fulfilling the terms of the treaty, Frederick wanted to assert his claims in northern Italy, especially against the centralizing tendencies of Milan, a city that our poet sees as an oppressive force. Frederick was also able to meet with specialists in Roman law from the university at Bologna (vv. 452-503), who could show him how to use its legal principles to enhance his authority. He also hoped to attack the Norman kingdom, as both the pope and rebel barons in Apulia were urging him to do.

Except for the coronation, which was performed by Eugenius' successor, Adrian IV, the first expedition was a failure. Lombardy was not subjugated. In spite of an open rebellion in southern Italy, his small army had stayed in Italy too long, and it was too weakened by malaria to take advantage of the situation. Despite the victory of Henry the Lion over the Roman commune on coronation day (vv. 689-759), he was unable to secure Rome for the pope, who was earlier disenchanted by the emperor's failure to follow etiquette and hold the pope's stirrup at their initial meeting before the coronation. After his departure, Adrian made a pact with the Norman king, which Barbarossa considered to be a violation of the Treaty of Constance.

XVIII

The second expedition consisted of a much larger force, which he planned to use to dominate northern Italy and to punish the pope and the Normans. But the result was not all that he had hoped. The invasion of the Norman kingdom never took place, and his papal policy did little more than perpetuate a schism, which resulted from a disputed election after the death of Pope Adrian in 1159. Split as to who should be his successor, the college of cardinals elected Rolando Bandinelli, a canon lawyer, who took the name Alexander III. But a minority of its members, encouraged by Barbarossa, selected another candidate, who was given Frederick's sanction during an ecclesiastical council that he organized at Pavia in 1160. The time, however, when emperors could make popes was over. The schism lasted almost two decades and put Frederick at a disadvantage, since most of Europe and especially the north Italian city-states supported Alexander.

Of all this, there is no mention in the poem. Instead, our author focuses on the events in northern Italy, where Frederick was more successful. Once he had coerced Milan and the other cities that opposed him, he used the Diet of Roncaglia in 1158 to demand prerogatives that could have reduced Lombardy to an imperial province. The poet rightly considers this edict to be the high point of Frederick's rule in northern Italy and describes it as the emperor's vehicle for establishing peace and justice (vv. 2597-2616). But, encouraged by the papacy and suspicious of the Roncaglian edicts, some of the communes rose in a futile revolt that the poet attributes to the prompting of a demon from Vergil's *Aeneid*, the fury Allecto (vv. 2629-35). The insurrection was unsuccessful and ended in the destruction of Milan in 1162, the last year of Frederick's second expedition. It is during this rebellion, at the battle of Carcano in 1160, that the poem ends.

Yet the period of Frederick's victories in Italy was itself coming to an end. In 1167, his march on Rome failed to capture Alexander, and his army was struck by malaria, which also killed Rainald of Dassel, his chancellor and perhaps the inspiration behind this poem. Since Frederick was now compelled to flee across the Alps, the north Italian city-states gained the courage to form an anti-imperial alliance called the Lombard League, to rebuild Milan, and, in 1168, to construct a fortress in western Lombardy named Alessandria after the pope. Because our poet was probably from Bergamo, one of the cities that joined the league, it has been speculated that this poem, so filled with praise for the emperor, was written before 1167. At any rate, Frederick's luck in Italy continued to sour. In 1176 he was defeated by the Lombard League at Legnano, and in the next several years made peace with both the papacy and the cities. Although the emperor could not dominate the peninsula, his Italian campaigns did not go entirely unrewarded. He was able to collect a healthy subsidy from Lombardy and to establish a power base in Tuscany.

He still had great power and prestige when news reached Europe in 1187 that Jerusalem had fallen to Moslem forces. Frederick, along with the kings of France and England, vowed to free the Holy City. The emperor, who led the largest contingent, took the overland route, and in 1190 in what is now Turkey, he fell from his horse in a rapidly moving stream and drowned. In later times, a legend, which had originally grown up around his grandson Frederick II, developed about him. Frederick, it claimed, did not die in the Near East, but rather he sleeps in a cave, to be awakened by the call of ravens when Germany again will need him.

II. THE AUTHOR

Clues to his Identity

Although the poem was written by an anonymous author, there are clues to his identity in the text itself. For example, he was a contemporary of Frederick Barbarossa because he tells us that he composed it or wished to compose it in Frederick's presence:

> I try things that are worthy of this prince,
> Whose presence will give strength to my attempt.   (4-5)

Was he a poet who lived and worked at the imperial court? He mentions that he was an eyewitness to the emperor's first siege of Milan:

> Right there I saw our leader's splendid tents,
> Which barely stood beyond the range of missiles....
> (2268-69)

The poet was obviously a well-educated man to undertake a Latin epic, written in almost errorless dactylic hexameters, and the poem shows his close acquaintance with many of the classics, including nearly the complete works of Vergil, Ovid, Statius, Horace, and Lucan.[2] He may well have been a student or professor at Bologna, since he gave us a vivid description of Frederick's visit to that city, but there is no hard evidence.

Was he a cleric?[3] Although his biblical references are few (there are only five), they are hardly commonplace. His use of paradigms, like the sons of Jonadad (vv. 2171-74), or King David after seeing Ziklag in ruins (vv. 2880-88), shows more than a superficial knowledge of the Book. Since it took eight lines to explain his simile about Ziklag, he did not expect his audience to understand it. If the poet were a layman, he knew his Bible. But, is the classical raiment in which the poem is garbed evidence of secularization? It would be an important indication of the poet's world view, only if we knew what value the author placed upon classical culture. The men of the twelfth century did not uniformly believe that a knowledge of ancient literature was harmful to Christian standards.[4] In addition, Erwin Panofsky considered the medieval use of classical themes and models to be governed by what he called the "principle of disjunction":

> Wherever in the high and later Middle Ages a work of art borrows its form from a classical model, this form is almost invariably invested with a non-classical, normally Christian significance; wherever in the high and later Middle Ages a work of art borrows its theme from classical poetry, legend, history or mythology, this theme is quite invariably presented in a non-classical, normally contemporary form.[5]

Moreover, since there is no evidence that the poet saw politics as a sphere independent from religion, his interest in it, like his interest in the classics, does not argue against a clerical status.

The manuscript has a northern Italian provenance, which is probably a clue to the poet's origin.[6] Internal evidence also links the poet to northern Italy. He praised the famous fishing grounds of the Lago d'Iseo and described the exact position of the castle at Trezzo. He could name the gates of Crema and knew that Mura was on the border of Bergamo and Brescia.[7]

He was probably from Bergamo,[8] a small commune to the northeast of Milan, which looked to the empire for support against the aggression of her larger neighbors, especially Brescia, which had been encroaching on the eastern part of her territory since the beginning of the century.[9] Certainly the poet had a great interest in the often violent rivalry between Bergamo and Brescia, which is of questionable importance to our understanding of the main conflict between Frederick and Milan. We are given a long and partisan account of their battle at Palosco, as well as a detailed description of the events concerning the conquest and reconquest of Volpino. Besides Henry the Lion and Frederick himself, the only individual mentioned during the battle at Rome was Manfred, a descendant of the ancient counts of Bergamo. A tenth of the entire poem and almost four-tenths of Book II were devoted to the history of that commune.[10]

In addition, since Barbarossa's success enhanced the declining position of the bishop within Bergamo, it is probable that the imperial partisan who wrote the poem was connected to the episcopal court. Gerard (1146-67), the bishop during the period in which the poem was probably composed, was an advocate of Frederick and supported his second marriage to Beatrice of Burgundy in 1156 (vv. 1104-16), in spite of the emperor's failure to have papal approval.[11] The bishop was rewarded, for in that year, Frederick increased the size of his diocese. Gerard's deposition in 1167 was probably related to the anti-imperial stance that Bergamo took at that time. Of the four major candidates for authorship, only Thaddeus of Rome, a completely unknown figure, has no demonstrable connection to the diocese. The other three, Teutaldus of Carvico, John Asinus of Gandino, and Moses of Brolo, all have ties to the episcopal court.

Thaddeus of Rome was the choice of the scholar who examined the question most recently, Irene Schmale-Ott, who completed the edition of this poem for the Monumenta Germaniae Historica.[12] In a scholium to his *Privilegia ac iura imperii* (1414) Dietrich of Niem mentions a poem about Frederick's wars with Milan, written by Master Thaddeus of Rome, who was present at a siege of Milan.[13] But Dietrich describes the siege as lasting four years, and since none of Barbarossa's attacks on the city lasted so long, Dietrich's information is muddled. In any case, although it would be satisfying to have the author's name, the real advantage of such information would derive from what it could impart about his life. The knowledge of his class, his education, and his career would give us a better understanding of his work and perhaps the society that produced him. But Thaddeus of Rome is just a name, and if it belonged to the author, it merely burdens us with another inconvenient fact, a place of origin that is at variance with the evidence of the poem and that, in turn, needs to be explained.

Teutaldus is perhaps the weakest candidate.[14] Wilhelm Gundlach argued that the poet gives undue importance to the siege of Volpino, in his view a relatively minor event, and this exaggerated emphasis can best be explained by postulating that the author had some connection to that place. He selected Teutaldus, a canon from S. Alessandro, the cathedral chapter that was considered to be pro-imperial. He came from neighboring Carvico, and his family had property in Volpino. The siege of Volpino, however, may have had greater importance than Gundlach thought, and in any case, the emphasis given to the episode can be explained by the poet's presence there during the siege or in a number of other ways.

The episcopal chancellor of Bergamo, John Asinus of Gandino, is a likely candidate. Most probably he had the intellectual background that would have been necessary to compose this poem, and there is a curious passage in Book III:

> Since John Gandino did not take the oath,
> He hastened to the king with rapid steps
> To tell how Brescia lawlessly constrained them. (1332-34)

If this oath is the one by which the Bergamasks were forced by Brescia to renounce their possession of Volpino in 1156, as it seems probable, then the poet may be lying because a list of a thousand Bergamasks who took the oath contains two Johns from Gandino. According to Angelo Mazzi, the poet is John Asinus of Gandino, and he was lying to protect an oath breaker, the other John of Gandino, who may have been a relative.[15] The debate over this issue is complicated because scholars often confused the two Johns, and this confusion led some to believe that John Asinus, the episcopal chancellor, would have been too old to write the poem.[16] But he remains a viable candidate since later research has shown that he died in the early thirteenth century, well after the probable date of composition.[17]

Perhaps the most attractive possibility is Moses of Brolo, a local scholar who was the author of a poem about

XXV

Bergamo, the *Liber Pergaminus*, and a remarkable linguist who served as the Greek interpreter to Emperor Lothar on his visit to Constantinople in 1134. Although some disagree, a number of scholars maintain that there are stylistic similarities between Moses' work and the Barbarossa epic.

Wilhelm von Giesebrecht[18] called our poet a possible student of Moses, and Joseph Sturm[19] asserted that both men were connected to a northern Italian school of poetry that was centered in Pavia. In addition, Moses was a friend of Ambrose, bishop of Bergamo from 1111 to 1131, and he also had a brother Pietro, who was the provost of the chapter of S. Alessandro. But, since Moses was most active in the 1130s and showed himself to be mature in his studies at that time, most scholars consider him too old to have written this poem thirty years later. Damien van der Eynde, however, discovered a letter that was probably written by Moses during the pontificate of Adrian IV (1154-59), some time after May or June 1156, and this evidence forbids us to ignore him as the possible author.[20] In 1920, Haskins attempted to attribute several works to Moses of Brolo, but *Barbarossa in Italy* was not among them.[21] Yet, it may be possible now that Moses cannot be disqualified because of age for some future philologists to find Grecisms or some other stylistic clues in the poem that would allow us to ascribe it to him.

Like so many facets of this work, the problem of authorship evokes more questions than answers. Even the assumption that the poet was connected to the episcopal court, although probable, is challenged by the positive image given to the bishop's chief rival in the city, the communal government. So, we are left only with hypotheses, some of which are ingenious, but none of which is wholly satisfactory.

III. The Title

The poem has no title, but there are two explicits beneath the text on the last page, neither of which is contemporary with the body of the work. The only complete one reads: "Here concludes the exploits of Frederick Barbarossa in Lombardy and Italy."

The poem has been given many names since its discovery, and some of them are based upon the explicit. The Trivulziana manuscript was titled *Frederici Aenobarbi gesta;*[22] and it has been called *Gesta di Federico I in Italia, Die Märe von Mailands Eroberung,*[23] *Carmen de Frederico I. imperatore,*[24] and *Carmen de gestis Frederici I. imperatoris in Lombardia.*

I find all these titles unsuitable for an English translation; and the last, the MGH version, is too cumbersome to be used in the text and not particularly accurate. Although the word "Lombardy" is found in one explicit, it is not a term that poet ever used. He wrote "Liguria," not "Lombardy," when he mentioned that imperial province south of the Alps whose boundaries were coterminous with neither modern Liguria nor modern Lombardy. I have therefore decided to call my translation *Barbarossa in Italy,* since it is concise and fits easily into the body of the text. The use of the word "Italy" is in one sense too general, because the action is centered in the northern part of that country, and in another sense it is too specific, because some of the events took place in northern Europe, i.e., Poland. Yet it captures the essence of the poem, and it is true to the explicit as well.

IV. The Time of Composition
and Length

Like its author and title, the exact time of the poem's composition is a matter of speculation. Since we know that it was written by a contemporary of Frederick I, the date of the manuscript, which is a later copy, is no help.[25] The poem was probably begun after the destruction of Milan in April of 1162, for the sixth verse speaks of Milan in the past tense ("There was a city...").[26] Later (v. 3144) the poet seemed to anticipate its capture when he stated that the refugees from Crema fled to Milan only to be conquered again, and in Gundlach's opinion, this must be a reference to the siege that led to Milan's fall.[27] The action of the poem does move in that direction, because from its beginning there is a slowly rising tension that seems to pull the two main protagonists, Frederick and Milan, toward some cataclysmic event. The destruction of the city would have made an artistically and psychologically satisfying conclusion for an imperial partisan.

According to Gundlach, the fall of Milan might have inspired the author to begin his poem immediately, and if he worked in Italy in the imperial presence, he would have started between April 1 and August 27, 1162. There is no evidence that a Bergamask contingent was present at the final siege of Milan, but since all Lombardy was supposed to be there, we may assume their participation. The poet may have stopped writing in 1166, because in that year Bergamo detached itself from the imperial camp, and in 1167 it decisively passed to the side of cities hostile to Frederick. Is it inconceivable that a patriotic Bergamask could continue writing a song of praise to the emperor under those circumstances?

There is no scholarly agreement on why the manuscript is in a seemingly uncompleted state. Giesebrecht cited the unpolished state of the text, i.e., repetitions of the same verse, as evidence that the poet, having lost his audience, left the poem unfinished. Other scholars, however, have maintained that the scribe never completed the extant copy and point to missing capital letters and an inconsistent use of red ink for decoration, among other things, to support their position. Schmale-Ott also noted that the expensive parchment was used in a wasteful manner, quite untypical of a medieval scribe, if in fact he knew in advance that the work would end where it does.[28]

How long might the poem have been? Schmale-Ott based her estimate on the amount of parchment that she postulated the scribe had available to him. If he used it all, she claims, the poem would be 4,300 verses in length, not the present 3,343.[29] Likewise, Dietrich Becker concluded that the poem was originally 4,160 lines long through his study of the work's content and organization.[30] Thus an analysis of both the physical manuscript and its contents brings us to the conclusion that the poem lacks between 800 and 900 verses, if it was indeed completed.

V. The Poet as Historian

In order to evaluate the poem's historical importance, it is proper to begin with a discussion of the poet's goals, since the task that he undertook has no precise modern equivalent. He wrote history insofar as he could accurately reconstruct the past, and empirical history insofar as he could gather his material from his own experience and eyewitnesses. His choice of poetry as a means of expression need not detract from his scholarly purpose, since didactic poems were common in both the ancient and medieval worlds.

Yet he conceived of his discipline more loosely than his modern counterparts, because he considered himself free to use imagination to supplement his sources and even to create a mythological character. Also he wrote history from which moral lessons were meant to be drawn, for his task had an ethical and an aesthetic purpose to which "scientific" accuracy was only a handmaiden.

The poem itself is a narration of Frederick's first two Italian campaigns. It begins with his election to the throne in 1152, and it ends abruptly in August of 1160. Since the poet was selective in the events that he narrated, it is not a complete account of these expeditions, but from what can be checked in other sources, the poet was usually accurate in describing the events that he chose to relate.[31]

Around 1,400 verses or about 40 percent of what remains has no parallel in other sources, and in addition to these, there are individual passages only to be found in the poem within incidents that were reported in other works.[32] It is one of the earliest, if less detailed, independent sources of Frederick's Italian journeys, and it should have equal stature with the *Gesta Frederici* of Otto of Freising and his continuator, Rahewin.[33]

Does the literary nature of the work affect its historical accuracy? As stated above, the poet did use fictional devices, like the fury Allecto and a dream sequence where Milan personified as an elegant old woman appears to Frederick. Yet it is usually easy to separate fact from fiction. This would not be true of battle scenes, which often resemble each other as well as those in the *Aeneid*, and which would have to be used with great caution.[34] One could still learn much about medieval warfare, such as the types of war machines used in a siege, from the poem.[35]

But the poem's value as a historical source goes beyond the factual accuracy of the narration. It is a testament to the modes of thought and feeling of a sensitive and intelligent partisan of Frederick I and the society that he reflected.[36] Yet the poet brought more to his art than a loyalty to his emperor, because he is capable of writing with a rare impartiality and sensitivity to the position of those with whom he disagreed. For example, Milan of course is the villain of the poem; the city was both arrogant and deceitful, and medievals considered those characteristics to be the roots of treason and traditionally associated with the vice of malice.[37] But the Bergamo master recognized local patriotism as a virtue that ennobled even the emperor's opponents, and communal government too was seen as legitimate and not incompatible with imperial rule.[38] The poet was able to show such sympathy toward Milan that Antonio Pagano calls this work a historical, not a heroic, poem, an impartial and truthful narration of Frederick's first two trips to Italy.[39] Milan, without the poet wanting it, becomes the hero of this poem, claims Angelo Monteverdi, although he admitted that the spirit of the poem is Ghibelline.[40] According to Becker the poet saw the conflict between Frederick and Milan as a struggle between two different types of order.[41] He might have been thinking of verses such as these:

> Imperial glory and the royal power
> As well as ancient grudges urged them on.
> The other side was moved by love of country,
> And the sweetness of the native soil helped.   (2327-30)

There was no question, however, on which side the greater right resided. To make that point as forcefully as he could, the poet places these words into the mouth of an enemy of Frederick, a Milanese consul:

> The Roman leader has the legal right,
> If we but speak the truth, to govern us.[42]   (2509-10)

His fair-mindedness is also evident in his delineation of Barbarossa. Frederick is the hero who wants to implement a program based upon the Vergilian values of peace and justice, and in his introductory portrait of the emperor, the poet attributes to him characteristics that conform to the medieval topos of ideal ruler:[43]

> He was pious and unequaled as a soldier
> And descended from an ancient line of kings.
> A wondrous legacy of strength and wisdom
> Was biform nature's double gift to him.   (57-60)

In fact, the Bergamo master stands close in sentiment to Otto and Rahewin in establishing the emperor's power on a theological and Roman base. According to him, Barbarossa was selected by God for the throne ("elected by the kindly nod of heaven"), and his coronation by Pope Adrian IV ("a man known for his character and learning"), was the one major event concerning Frederick's relationship with the papacy that the poet wanted to relate. Twice he writes that Frederick received the crown from "consecrated hands."[44] The quarrel between the pope and the emperor at Sutri before the coronation and the later schism were both suppressed. Religiosity was one of the important characteristics of the Italian medieval epic, and *Barbarossa in Italy* was true to its genre.[45] According to one commentator, *romanitas* was Frederick's most secure base of authority in the poem.[46] His role as the restorer of Roman power was probably as important as his capacity to pacify the Italian city-states. The poet continually refers to him as Roman king and Roman emperor. Miracles supported the imperial cause, and the poet speaks of the ancient authority of Rome with an almost religious fear:

> The world once lived in fear of Roman power:
> In places where the sun would rise and set
> No people spurned the emperor's commands
> Unless they wished to forfeit all respect.
> But now some in Liguria test our might,
> And in their pride they violate our honor.   (1509-14)

Frederick is the embodiment of kingly virtue, but he is more human than, for example, Charlemagne in the *Song of Roland*, who has in D. W. Robertson's view: "not the depth and fullness of a human personality, but the depth and fullness of an idea."[47] Frederick was capable of making a tragic mistake out of anger and ignorance. He ordered hostages to be bound to a siege machine and allowed them to be stoned to death by the defenders of Crema, an action of which he is not proud:

> He moved the tower back and freed the wretches.
> Too late he scorned advice he took in anger.   (3029-30)

The poet's fairness can also be seen in his treatment of Arnold of Brescia. His description of Arnold's teaching and his death are quite sympathetic. The account of his execution has the greatness of the *passio* of a martyr, commented

Arsenio Frugoni.[48] Ferdinand Gregorovius noted that according to the poet Frederick regretted ordering his death,[49] but in the passage that follows the regret was reserved for the loss of a brilliant man who wasted his talents, not for the execution itself, which was a necessity. The indication of sorrow was just a way of showing the emperor's compassion. The poet sympathetically articulates Arnold's criticism of clerical abuses, but his strong interest in reestablishing peace and order in Italy prevented him from supporting an attack on the institutional Church itself. However much admiration he felt for Arnold, his final judgment on his teaching was negative.[50]

The passage about Arnold, which was placed after the coronation scene and the battle for Rome, was probably meant to illustrate Frederick's concern for sound doctrine and his ability to work in harmony with the Church. Of course it was also a criticism of Bergamo's rival, Brescia:

> Then Arnold was residing in those regions,
> Whom Brescia bore and honored overmuch.   (760-61)

Yet the episode was handled with such skill and understanding that one might well believe him to be a supporter of Arnold if the thrust of the poem did not work against that view. This use of sympathetic imagination makes for high drama and prevents lopsided historiography.[51]

In addition to his sensitivity and fairness, the poet's mind was shaped by an intelligence that made him more than a reporter of unconnected attitudes and events. He wished to understand why people act as they do, and the will to delve into the thought behind the action is, according to R. G.

Collingwood, the key to historical knowledge.[52] For example, the speeches of Allecto are more than literary devices that propel the action forward; they are documents that give us insight into the reasons why the communes revolted against Frederick. Allecto was imaginary, but the fears that she played upon were real. According to Becker, her speech to Crema reflected exactly its concern for its own security under the peace that was established at Roncaglia in 1158.[53] If these speeches never give the text of what is said, asserted Schmale-Ott, they almost always give the meaning.[54]

The poet was also concerned with the motivation of individuals, for in his narration of the siege of Trezzo, he paused to examine the motives of Vintelmo for deserting the fort:

> He either feared
> Milan's destruction, or as rumor had it,
> He had thought to cheat in a nefarious way.
> Could he gain more by feigning to change sides?
> Or perhaps the greedy man expected presents? (2176-80)

The Bergamo master possessed a complex view of the past. On the one hand he did not deny transcendental order, since he affirmed that destiny is on the side of the emperor, and that only the foolish rebel against fate. Speaking of the Milanese, he states:

> How ignorant is man of what must be.
> How badly he foresees his disappointments. (326-27)

On the other hand, fortune or luck had her role to play:

> Thus fortune varies. Thus the high and low
> Will change their places when she spins her wheel.
>
> (441-42)

But people were not merely the playthings of unseen powers, and the historical process was not a simplistic morality play in which they were reduced to puppets who acted according to roles given to them. Events grew out of circumstances and people responding to actions of others in an almost dialectical manner. This attitude brought the poet closer to a modern conception of historical reality than any of his contemporaries. The future belonged to this kind of history writing.[55]

History, then, was a fabric of intricate design. It was not completely intelligible, for humans with all their strengths and weaknesses participated in it under the mysterious guidance of Providence. These are the assumptions that our author brought to his work as a historian, and they help to make it, in Giovanni Cremaschi's words, *un prezioso documento* (a precious document).[56]

VI. LITERARY SIGNIFICANCE

Barbarossa in Italy is an example of a literary genre that was common to medieval Italy, the Latin historical epic. This type of literature developed almost without interruption from the ninth century and reached its apex in the eleventh and twelfth centuries.[57] In fact, while the Bergamo master was writing *Barbarossa in Italy,* an anonymous Milanese may have been composing a poem, also epic in tone and classical in inspiration, on the same topic. Written between 1162 and 1167, it was called the *De destructione civitatis Mediolanensis.*[58]

These works were based upon historical events and written in Latin by poets who lived close to the period that they were describing. Therefore these epics are unlike their more famous counterparts from north of the Alps, to which they are often unfavorably compared. For example, poems like the *Song of Roland* were said to show great creativity in the use of language and in their plots, because they were written in the emerging vernacular and not caught in the palsied grasp of the classical tradition, and because they were based upon old legends that could be freely adapted. The poet could blend his imagination with those of past generations to write a vivid, highly creative tale.

Monaci himself had strong misgivings about the literary quality of the poem he had discovered.[59] He believed that *Barbarossa in Italy* made an important contribution to historical science, but that it had little merit as a work of art. Monaci asked Giesebrecht to evaluate it only as a historical document, and he in turn had almost nothing to say about its artistic value. This prejudice against the poem has found its way into the literature. In Germany the major questions raised about this work have been of a historical nature, and there has been little interest in its literary merit.[60] In Italy most scholars of the poem have commented on its artistic significance, but many have done so unfavorably. Criticisms fall into three categories. (1) Since history is incompatible with imaginative literature, the poem is merely a versified chronicle of no artistic value. (2) The poet's dependence on classical literature was too great, for it stifled his creativity and led to an awkwardness of style. (3) The third criticism is almost a mirror image of the second: the poem's adherence to medieval artistic canons works against its effectiveness as epic literature.

History and Art

To Monteverdi history was incompatible with art, and our poet's historical preoccupation killed every artistic possibility. According to him, the Bergamo master has given us only a chronicle gilded with verse.[61] Yet, it is clear from even a superficial reading of the poem that the author was writing more than a versified chronicle, a dry recitation of facts in turgid poetry that was concocted for some legal or historical purpose. He was a gifted storyteller who was creating a work of literature that was meant to play on the emotions of his audience and to involve them in the plot.[62] At times the poet addresses them directly and gives the impression of an immediate fantastic reconstruction of events:

> Now watch the missiles break the walls apart
> And shatter houses, while frightened peasants run.
>
> (371-72)

An epic is, after all, a war story, and the Bergamo master wanted it to be sufficiently gory to titillate his public:

> They crushed their chests, their stomachs and their heads,
> And bone and mushy brain were mixed together.
>
> (3024-25)

He also attempted to keep the reader's attention through elaborate descriptions, like the detailed account of the location of the fortress at Trezzo, and the people's elation at Frederick's return to Italy:

> A woman long deprived of her dear husband
> Was kissed as she had wished for many days.
> All gave their thanks and praised the Lord of Heaven.
> They celebrated at a joyous banquet....   (1096-99)

XXXVIII

The use of metaphors was also important to our author. Most of these came from family life and nature:[63]

> Just so a hostile band of wolves will feast
> By trapping and attacking herds of cattle.　　(1851-52)

Above all the use of orations, which comprise about one quarter of the poem, injected life into the narrative. The Bergamo master had the ability to integrate them into the story so that they enhance our understanding and enjoyment without slowing the pace. The speeches of the fury Allecto to the rebellious Lombard communes, in books four and five, are perhaps the highlights of the poem. The daemon is a mistress of psychology, who is able to manipulate the personal and political fears of her victims to rekindle the war.

Since anyone who has studied history seriously must feel the drama latent in it, a historical theme need not detract from the literary nature of the work.[64] In addition, because medieval artists were accustomed to use an inherited body of material with themes based upon old legends or topoi transmitted from the ancient world, an original story was hardly a necessity for a work of literature.[65] A historical subject could serve as well any other. As Peter Dronke points out, the medieval artist's individuality can be found precisely in the way that he handles a traditional body of material.[66]

In comparison to historical characters, purely fictional creations have greater freedom to express what the author wishes to say. Yet the artist who chooses a historical theme is able to select that part of the past that makes his point. Then if he wishes to remain true to the historical record, he must exploit the dramatic potential that is intrinsic in the actual situation. Although his characters have limited freedom of movement, still he must use his imagination. But it must be a disciplined imagination, grounded in the circumstances in which the actors find themselves, and they must act in a way that is consistent with the character and the situation itself.[67] In this way an artist can produce an image of the past that is perhaps truer than the one created by a historian who is limited to his sources. It can be as vivid as a purely fictional work, whose characters must touch reality, if they are to touch us.

The reality of a twelfth-century imperial partisan, his basic assumptions about the nature of the world, however, was such that he could never draw a picture of his emperor that a modern reader would find wholly acceptable. But our poet did have the imaginative power to create scenes that were dramatically effective and consistent with the historical record. For example, when the Milanese approached Frederick on his first visit to Italy, they were anxious to win him to their side, and they addressed him as the king of Rome, a title that implied the universality of his rule. But when they stood in rebellion against him, he was greeted:

> O red-haired ruler of the German fury,
> Turn from this path. You have no right to cross
> The Adda, which protects our sacred nation....
>
> (2086-88)

This attitude mirrors that of John of Salisbury, whose hostility to Barbarossa prevented him from referring to Frederick as Roman emperor and caused him to emphasize his German ethnicity instead.[68] Therefore the address has dramatic impact, and it is historically credible.

Since the poet used his imagination to enhance the drama, he clearly did not write a versified chronicle, but can he still be criticized for following a chronicler's means of organization? It is not that time considerations are so important; events are not simply lumped together chronologically. But like many a medieval chronicler, did he only report the events that appealed to him? What were the principles that formed the basis of his selectivity? Did he show an artist's sense of economy of detail or a historian's sense of relevance?

The theme of the poem, as stated above, is the conflict between Frederick and Milan, and the sense of this struggle wove itself into the very fabric of the verse. In his analysis of the siege of Crema, Becker noted that there was little use of enjambment, because the poet wanted us to see the power of the conflict through a series of constant changes.[69] Indeed, throughout the poem there are times when lines seem to clash against each other, to push in opposite directions:

> They used what means they had to stop their foes,
> But the tortoise could repel the rain of blows....
>
> (3044-45)

Also unity of theme was attained by an often judicious selection of events, which were chosen because of the way in which they gave artistic expression to some phase of the struggle.[70] Subplots and digressions were usually subordinated to the main story. For example, the rivalry between Brescia and Bergamo was depicted as part of the larger confrontation, with Bergamo appearing as loyal to the emperor and with Brescia as loyal to Milan. Gundlach saw the poem as more tightly constructed than the *Ligurinus,* with only the marriage to Beatrtice not relevant to the story. In his estimation the interlude in Poland can be justified by the Polish duke's participation in the second Italian expedition.[71] In this case the marriage scene can also be explained, since Beatrice herself brought an army to Italy.

In spite of these arguments, however, the poet does not seem to have escaped entirely from a method of selection that was at times personal and somewhat arbitrary. For example, after the episode in Poland the Polish duke disappeared from the text, and his importance to the expedition above the others is unclear, since according to Rahewin, he did not participate in the Italian campaign.[72] The meeting of Barbarossa with the academics of Bologna is meant to enhance the emperor's image by showing him as a patron of scholars. But it is an unnecessary departure from the main theme. Since the poem is principally about men and a man's business, war, the marriage scene may have to do with the poet's desire to introduce a female character for variety, and to follow his model, Vergil. Aeneas had his Dido or, better, his Lavinia. But the account of Frederick's Italian campaign would not have been weakened without it.

Yet to see the poem as a hodgepodge of random events is to miss the poet's ability as a storyteller. He has taken different events for different motives, and although in some cases their integration with the main theme is less successful than in others, the net effect has been to create a well-told tale with plenty of tension.

The Classical Tradition

Has the poet relied too heavily on the classics? Is *Barbarossa in Italy* the poem of a man who sought to find in the work of others words he himself could not provide? Monaci calls it a mosaic, consisting of lines and parts of lines from ancient authors clumsily linked together, and supports his argument by the notes to his edition, where page after page is filled with citations to classical texts.[73] His opinion, however, ignores the originality with which the poet constructed his verse, and Monaci's examples of borrowing are usually based on the common use of only one or two words. Certainly, the Bergamo master is inspired by classical Latin poetry and at times borrows lines from Vergil and other ancient poets, but there are narrow linguistic connections in only about one percent of the poem.[74] Sometimes there may be a reminiscence based upon a much earlier reading, or he may have created a similar phrase himself. In general the poet's words are his own.

If in his verse the poet demonstrated the ability to use his classical background in an original way, the same is true in his handling of the contents. He could tell a moving tale that is free of prototypes, like the Arnold of Brescia episode,[75] but like a Romanesque architect who employed the Roman arch to construct a very un-Roman building, the Bergamo master could take ancient models as points of departure for his own creative activity. Certainly he believed that he had found a striking parallel between his own age and the world of the *Aeneid*. Like Aeneas, Frederick was a foreigner who had come to Italy to establish Roman rule, to bring peace and justice. But in spite of similarities between the two epics, our poet did rush in where Vergil feared to tread by writing directly about his hero, rather than by praising him indirectly in a poem about his ancestors.[76] Likewise, the Bergamo master borrowed the fury Allecto from Vergil, but he used her according to his own requirements, a good example of his dependence upon and yet his willingness to stray from classical sources.

This is also true of the sequence in which Milan, personified as an elegant, elderly woman, appeared to Frederick while he was sleeping in his camp in the fields outside of Verona. The idea was borrowed from Lucan's *De bello civili*, where Caesar met Rome personified as a woman just before he crossed the Rubicon. But the speech, dress, and deportment of the two women as well as the denouement is not the same.[77] In fact, Ernst Curtius has traced the medieval topos of the vital old woman back to early Christian literature, but he believed that its true origin is "the stock of archaic proto-images in the collective unconscious."[78] Also Caesar's vision comes to him while his eyes are open. It is something surprising, unexpected, beyond the experience of reality.[79] By placing Frederick's vision in a dream, the poet gave it a verisimilitude that the other lacks, and it is in keeping with the historical nature of the poem where even a fantastic creature like Allecto used natural means to attain her goals.

The poet could mix the classical and the Christian in a way that saw no tension between the two. For example, there is the description of Frederick's bride:

> For Venus did not have this virgin's beauty;
> Minerva did not have her brilliant mind,
> And Juno did not have her wealth. There never
> Was another except God's Mother Mary,
> And Beatrice is so happy She excels her.   (1110-14)

Monteverdi found this passage eccentric because of its juxtaposition of the classical and the Christian.[80] But the passage merely reflects a common medieval literary theme that Curtius called the topos of outdoing.[81] Surely the goddesses as religious symbols died long before the poem was written. They posed no threat to the Virgin, for they are simply standards of feminine perfection to be compared unfavorably with Frederick's bride, who herself stands beneath Mary. Christian and classical meet with charming effect.

The writings of T. S. Eliot and Ezra Pound have made twentieth-century readers more receptive to the technique by which a poet may echo themes or even borrow lines from earlier works. It can be very effective, if done properly, especially for a man who wishes to link himself to a specific literary tradition. Writing about Pound's use of Homer in Canto I of the *Cantos*, Michael Alexander states:

> Like Eliot's recourse to Sanskrit in *The Waste Land*, it goes back to the original ground of knowledge for its author, a respectful if inquiring relation with nature and with the human past, gained through arduous submission. We ascend to the source of Western literature and wisdom in order to get our bearings.[82]

Medieval Style

Although we can hear a classical accent, the poet spoke the language of his times. He was influenced by the ornate, rhetorical style that flourished in the Middle Ages and that Curtius called mannerism. Among other things, the mannerist author often seeks complex ways of making simple points. For example, instead of telling his audience that it is the springtime, the Bergamo master resorts to this astronomical paraphrase, which Curtius cited as an example of mannerist circumlocution:[83]

Now Phoebus reached the limits of crouched Taurus
And saw that Gemini was rushing near.
The farmer now rejoiced to see his harvest,
And he prepared to give his thanks to God.   (1797-1800)

Also a mannerist author loves to manipulate language for its own sake in a way that the modern world often finds artificial. For example, this poem contains a creation like *Cardi etiam nales*, which might be considered an extraordinary example of hyperbaton.[84] Rhyming too is often thought to be bad form in an epic poem, and the Bergamo master used both caudate rhyming and the leonine verse, a technique of internal rhyming in which the first syllable of the third or fourth foot rhymes with the end syllable. There are twenty-two leonine verses in the first hundred lines.[85]

Do mannerist techniques work against the poem's effectiveness? The answer of course depends on who is asked, but the admiring Pagano's comment that the poem is so good that one would not believe it to be medieval literature if it were not on a medieval theme shows the antipathy against which it has had to labor.[86] Many scholars, however, would agree that it is anachronistic to apply classical standards to medieval poetry, and that the Bergamo master's verse is flowing and skillfully done by a man well prepared to approach his topic.[87]

The feudal epoch with its emphasis on military virtues was a fitting time to attempt an epic poem and not to have it sound artificial, even if the literary form was the product of an earlier age. Every work of art reflects the period of its creation and the stylistic canons that it prescribes. But we measure an artist's skill by the way he uses these techniques to interest and to excite, to touch the humanity of those who read him, and it is more to his credit if he can continue to involve his readers long after he is dust. By this standard *Barbarossa in Italy* is an exemplary work, a product of the Italian Romanesque, as sparkling as the mosaics in Santa Maria in Trastevere, and as full of life as those in San Clemente at Rome.

VII. THE PROBLEM OF HOHENSTAUFEN COURT HISTORIOGRAPHY

The longest and most hotly-debated controversy that this poem has generated had its origin in the attempt to discover the author's sources. The discussion eventually went beyond the poem to pose questions about the nature and purpose of all medieval literature that glorified a political leader. It started in the 1920s when Robert Holtzmann began research for his never-completed MGH edition of *Barbarossa in Italy*. He noted similarities in phrasing and parallels in narration that demonstrated a source-critical connection between the poem and the *Gesta Frederici* of Otto of Freising and his continuator, Rahewin.[88] There were many differences, however, and since these spoke against a direct use of the *Gesta* by the poet, Holtzmann postulated the existence of a now lost source that served as a basis *(Vorlage)* for both the *Gesta* and the poem, as well as several other works.

According to Holtzmann, Rahewin mentions this *Vorlage* in the prologue to his continuation of the *Gesta*, where he states that the *coeptum opus* and the *memoriale* of the famous man should not be allowed to perish. The *coeptum opus* (the work begun) is obviously the *Gesta*. The *memoriale* (a book containing records), however, is not a second expression for the same thing, as it had been commonly thought, but a reference to this lost source.

Holtzmann also contended that the authors of the *Gesta* and the Bergamo epic were not the only ones to benefit from this official presentation. In addition Gunther used it for the *Ligurinus,* and John of Cremona for his lost history, which served as the basis of the life of Frederick in the chronicle of Burchard of Ursberg.

The Holtzmann thesis received support from Walter Stach in two articles published in the late 1930s,[89] which gave a motive for this court-produced literature. According to Stach, the poems about Frederick are more than literary exercises that articulate generalized notions of medieval lordship; rather they are spiritual statements that give us insight into the thought processes of the contemporary political world. What then, he asked, was the ground of experience into which the individual works were rooted? What was the hidden political purpose of the authors.[90]

Stach asserted that there was an attempt to use poetry as a vehicle of imperial propaganda to counteract opinions hostile to Frederick emanating from other parts of Europe, for there is a striking similarity in the attitude of the Barbarossa poets towards foreign criticism of the empire.[91] In this poetry, he claimed, we have a song sung by a choir of voices that has the same melody, and all of these authors stood in official or in some other obligated relationship to the house of Hohenstaufen. They seem to have labored at the behest of a silent instruction, because their works generate a political feeling that appears to be somehow official. In Stach's opinion, Rainald of Dassel was the original architect of Barbarossa's image. It was he who took the concept of late

Roman absolutism and forged it into a strikingly powerful tool of imperial propaganda, and traces of his handiwork can be found in the literature of the period.

There were, however, serious objections to Holtzmann's theory raised by E. Ottmar,[92] who maintained that the similarities between the *Gesta* and *Barbarossa in Italy* were accidental. Since they were caused by a similar handling of the same theme, he argued, there is no need to postulate the existence of a now-lost *Vorlage*.

The discussion has continued for about sixty years, during which the most cogent comments were written by Franz-Josef Schmale in 1965.[93] According to him the debate between Holtzmann and Ottmar was settled largely in Ottmar's favor. Ottmar was essentially correct, he emphasized, because identical passages would have to exist in the works under consideration for Holtzmann to be persuasive, and anyway it is methodologically impossible to prove a lost common source if mutual use of the works in question cannot be excluded with certainty.

But Schmale thought Ottmar wrong to maintain that the source-critical relationships between works like the *Gesta* and *Barbarossa in Italy* were accidental. Different descriptions of the same events need not be cast in similar molds, as Ottmar believed. If one compares the literature discussed by Holtzmann to that which relates the same occurrences in a really independent manner, to the Milanese *Gesta*, to Vincent of Prague, or to Otto Morena, for example, one finds both the choice of words and narrative details to be different. In fact, the more unconnected the accounts, the greater the variation, so that at times it is almost impossible to establish the real facts.

But this is not true of works like the *Gesta* and *Barbarossa in Italy*. In spite of the different stylistic requirements of prose and poetry, there are not a few linguistic similarities, and they are to be found most often where there are parallels in the narrative. These too are striking, extending even to simulated speeches in the same places. In addition, the poet agreed with the *Gesta* in his report of events that lay beyond the possibility of his observation. Although the two authors are not always in harmony, the differences can be attributed to the supplementary knowledge available to each and to their individual personalities. But it can hardly be doubted that the Bergamo master knew and used the *Gesta*.

Therefore, Schmale concluded, the *Gesta* was also the source of the *Ligurinus*, and probably of Burchard's chronicle or of his lost source, John of Cremona.[94] It was fundamental to what Holtzmann considered to be Hohenstaufen court historiography, and without it three or four works would not have been written or not written in the manner that they were.

Was there nonetheless a court-directed attempt at political propaganda? If there was, Schmale argued, Frederick would have been the first German ruler to aim at a definite political journalism influenced by himself. It is probably better to consider the *Gesta* and related works as examples of courtly literature, rather than official histories based upon official documents. Although originally they may have had some other purpose, in the end they served only for the self-admiration of the emperor and the court, for if they were propaganda, every propagandistic effect was lacking. Except for the circle of authors around the court, there was little interest in them. In fact, Otto of Freising had more impact on modern times, especially the nineteenth century, than he did on his own day. Related works, like *Barbarossa in Italy*, all of which exist in only one manuscript copy, also had limited appeal in spite of the excellence of their authors.

Since Schmale's arguments failed to convince eminent scholars like Karl Langosch[95] or Horst Fuhrmann,[96] we might examine the problem again by asking what conclusions can be drawn from this scholarship that is often so contradictory.[97] First, most scholars who examined the problem in detail believed that parallels in language, narrative, or political concepts exist among the Barbarossa literature that they investigated. These commentators thought those parallels were not merely accidental, but that they derived from contact with the court or some work or individual associated with the court. Even Ottmar conceded that the mutual examination of the same documents might be responsible for a number of similarities in the texts.

Can we go farther and say there was a court-directed policy that helped to produce or shape this literature? Here the conclusions are mixed, but two questions may provide some insight. First, did the court have a plausible motivation to encourage such literature? Second, is there any evidence to show that the court actually did so?

Stach maintained that the answer to the first question is yes, because it was politically expedient for the court to manufacture propaganda. Becker considered such thinking to be anachronistic, and one may further ask: what was the value of written propaganda in a society that was largely illiterate, and whose government was not dependent on the popular will? It is also true that Stach's picture of the Hohenstaufen court often seemed to reflect his own era, the Germany of the late 1930s, more than the Middle Ages. For example, Barbarossa was depicted as a superman, or more precisely as one whose ability to face superhuman obligations *(übermenschlichen Verpflichtungen),* inspired Gunther and others.[98] Exempted from common moral standards, he would sweep Germany of foreign influence, as he restored her to her former greatness. He based his government on Germanic tradition: "There is only one law for Rome, whether she wants it or not, the German; only one single right, that of the German emperor; only one freedom, to serve the German king...."[99] Stach did not pursue this line of inquiry after the war.

But it is also true that institutions in all ages have attempted to influence people, and this admission does not call into question the sincerity or the high moral purpose of those involved. Gerd Tellenbach saw the Investiture Conflict as "the first medieval crisis to call forth a considerable propagandistic literature, in which the aims of the two parties were reflected."[100] Fuhrmann related that during the reign of Henry IV:

> Newsletters which dealt with current affairs circulated through the country and new doctrines were announced from the pulpit. Brunno describes how during the Easter sermon in Mainz in 1075, at which the king was present, a messenger entered with a letter from the Saxons, and demanded that it should be "read out and interpreted to all present" from the pulpit; when this was refused, the messenger himself explained the letter's contents to the people.[101]

Albert Brackmann saw the cult of the ruler as an integral part of the new centralized national state that first appeared in Norman lands and that served as a model for Frederick. This new emphasis on the person of the emperor is reflected "in the historical literature of the period."[102] This literature could be construed as political, but with Bulst's caveat that in the Middle Ages there was no such thing as purely political poetry, because there was no independent sphere of politics.[103]

The use of poetry need not be a drawback to propaganda literature, since the limitations of poetic expression have more to do with the ability of the poet than with the medium itself. Also to see poetry as merely reflecting the subjective world of the poet, as some scholars have done, is anachronistic. The ancients and medievals thought it adequate for both science and philosophy.

But Fuhrmann urged caution in evaluating the utility of what seems to be blatant propaganda, for it

> should always be borne in mind: terms like "pamphlet literature," "broadsheets," and "public debate" are used, but the manuscript transmission of many of these works is so meager that they can hardly have reached a wide public or had the function of a pamphlet or broadsheet in their own time.[104]

If there was a political use for the Barbarossa literature, the paucity of manuscripts argued against its success. To write, in part, out of political expediency may not have been beyond the ken of medievals but there is no evidence that this material was ever used as such. In addition, it is curious that *Barbarossa in Italy*, if it is propaganda, would report the atrocity at Crema and give such a positive image to communal

government, whose independence Frederick tried to curb at
the Diet of Roncaglia in 1158.

Yet, irrespective of the propaganda motive, it is still pos-
sible to maintain that the Barbarossa literature was court-
directed in a general way. There was a long-standing tradi-
tion, as ancient as Gilgamesh and Homer, that a great war-
rior or king has a right to bask in his own glory. Roland
began his first speech in the *Song of Roland* with a litany
to his prowess, and he recalls his feats of valor just before his
death.[105] Since soldiers and kings were often not men of
great verbal ability, a poet had an important role in helping
them praise themselves, and there was an early Germanic
tradition of celebrating contemporary leaders as well as
legendary personages.[106] Holtzmann asked "Had not
Charlemagne, in whom Frederick Barbarossa recognized his
model, been a focus for the spiritual interests of his time and
been praised by poets and historians?"[107] Thus it is possible
that there was a conscious policy on the part of Frederick to
cultivate his image, but his motives may have been those of
a warrior king (or of one who saw himself as such) and not
those of a modern demagogue.

Is there any evidence that could be used to support the
theory that this literature was court-directed? Rahewin stated
in his prologue that he was writing at the command of Otto
and "at the behest of the most serene and divine Emperor
Frederick...."[108] According to Becker, the context of this
passage shows that Rahewin is trying only to fulfill the wish
of the dead bishop and that he desires the express agreement
of the emperor.[109] The text does not allow for such an un-
ambiguous interpretation, but the tone of the imperial re-
quest takes on a less strident quality if it is separated from a

calculated master plan with a definite political goal. This would allow for a degree of sentimentality to be more easily mixed into Rahewin's motivation and give to the Bergamo master the freedom to develop his theme as he wished. The poet may have desired to educate the court about conditions in Italy as well as to praise the emperor.

If there was a conscious policy on the part of Frederick to cultivate his image, he may well have entrusted the direction of this task to his chancellor, Rainald of Dassel. Rainald had both the education and the enthusiasm to serve the emperor as his patron of the arts, and this is the role, not that of propaganda minister, which Holtzmann attributed to him.[110] Since Rainald did encourage Archpoet to write in praise of Frederick, he may have turned to others as well.

If one accepts this theory, the question then becomes what materials did Rainald and the authors whom he enlisted deem necessary to accomplish their task? Would Rainald have created an official presentation so closely based upon chancellery documents that Holtzmann and Langosch referred to it as a "collection of material" *(Materialsammlung)*?[111] A medieval writer would not rush to the archives when he wished to broach a historical topic, nor would he expect others to do so for him. He may well have used documents; Otto did, and Rahewin relied heavily upon them. But in neither case does their use of archival material seem intrinsic to their understanding of the historical discipline. For Otto a historian should be a witness to the events he describes:

> For it is said to have been a custom of the ancients that those who had perceived with their senses the actual

events as they took place should be the ones to write about them. Whence also it is customarily called "history" from *hysteron,* which in Greek signifies "to see." For everyone will be competent to speak more fully of the things which he has seen and heard. Being in need of no man's favor, he is not carried hither and thither in search of truth, dubiously anxious and anxiously dubious. Truly, it is hard for a writer's mind to depend on another's judgment, as though incapable of making an investigation of its own.[112]

In relating the events of the Council of Pavia, Rahewin stated that he was including letters and documents in the text to allow the reader to come to his own conclusions.[113] Most probably Rahewin did not desire to arrive at a judgment himself, since any opinion he might express would have been offensive to one side or the other, and so his inclusion of documents was simply a means of evasion.[114] Documents in the Middle Ages were used to establish or to defend legal rights, not to preserve the historical record in a modern sense.[115] Therefore the existence of an official chancellery presentation that would be systematically used by a number of authors, if not impossible, is at least improbable.

To an author like the Bergamo master, who lived through the period that he narrated, his own experience, both at court and elsewhere, as well as eyewitness accounts and other verbal reports, must have supplied an important part of the material that he used. These would have been supplemented by imperial letters and a work from the same literary rhetorical tradition as his poem, the *Gesta Frederici* of Otto and Rahewin.

VIII. This Edition

The discoverer of the poem, Ernesto Monaci, published an edition of it in 1887,[116] which helped to establish the text for a manuscript that had been damaged and was illegible in places. Although Monaci made a valuable contribution to our understanding of this epic, Giovanni Pesanti and S. T. Collins found many errors in his work.[117] Robert Holtzmann planned to contribute a new edition for the MGH in the 1920s, but it never appeared. The material he had prepared was destroyed during World War II, and Holtzmann himself died in 1946. The project was then reassigned to Irene Schmale-Ott, who published the MGH edition in 1965.[118] Although she profited from the work of previous scholars, she was also able to use modern technical equipment, like a quartz lamp, to decipher passages that were obscure to Monaci and to verify many of the emendations that Collins had made on the basis of meter. Langosch gave her edition a favorable review, admiring her thoroughness.[119] In 1985 J. B. Hall[120] questioned the accuracy of a number of her lines; but his recommendations often do no more than confirm the text Monaci had established originally. Although I have taken the objections of Hall and others into consideration, the Schmale-Ott edition is the principal source for my translation.

There was an incident in Frederick's career that underscores the importance of a translator. In October of 1157 two papal legates arrived at a diet that the emperor was holding at Besançon with a letter from Adrian IV, which complained that Frederick had been indifferent to the kidnapping of Bishop Eskil of Lund, and it contained a sentence that was construed to mean the pope was claiming feudal lordship over the emperor. The translator, Rainald of Dassel, had rendered the word *beneficia* as "fiefs" rather than by its less technical meaning of "favors" or "benefits." Rainald's interpretation caused a great commotion, and Otto of Wittelsbach is said to have threatened the legates' lives. A serious strain was placed upon the relationship between pope and emperor.

Although a medieval poem could not have such important political implications in the twentieth century, still the translator's art can make all the difference in the understanding of a work like *Barbarossa in Italy*, particularly in a society where the number of people who would undertake to read a Latin verse epic in the original is small indeed. Therefore I thought it worthwhile to discuss briefly the principles that guided me in making this translation.

First, I decided to render the 3,343 Latin verses into an equal number of English ones, although I have chosen to write in iambic pentameter, which has a sound that I believe is properly suited to an epic poem, but which is shorter than the Latin heroic verse, dactylic hexameter. This has caused me at times to compress and epitomize the text. Since I often use anacrusis and feminine endings to lengthen the line, I have tried to keep the loss of content to a minimum and in no way to distort the intent of the author. Because the poem is tied to the "mannerist" rhetorical tradition, I believe that this compression will be appealing to the modern reader who prefers clarity and directness of approach. In this I am following the example of Charles Mierow in his translation of the *Gesta* of Otto and Rahewin, who at times felt it necessary to compress his text.[121]

INTRODUCTION

Yet I have tried to capture some of the wordplay, the rhetorical tricks, and the love of the sound of words that were part of the aesthetic values of this poet and his era. The reader will find techniques like *annominatio*, the repetition of the same or homophonous words, *anaphora*, the repetition of the same or similar words at the beginning of successive verses, and other such techniques. Like the poet, I also use devices of sound like alliteration and consonance freely, and there is some internal and caudate rhyming. At times caudate rhyming is employed to finish a passage or to underline an aphorism. There is precedent in the Latin for such usage.

Since this is the first translation into English,[122] I have attempted to keep close to the original meaning of the text. But because "the purpose of poetical translation is the poetry, not the verbal definitions in dictionaries,"[123] the context, function of a line, the quality of the English verse, and the naturalness of the phrasing were important in shaping my translation. In a very few instances I have aimed at a similar rhetorical effect rather than at the literal meaning. Yet in no way did I try to write a poem about a poem, but rather the poem that our author himself would have written if he had been writing in English. Often I have tried to follow the advice that Ezra Pound gave to his German translator when he told him to translate what he meant, not what he said.

Therefore it is my hope that this translation could be used in a history or literature class as well as enjoyed by the educated reader. What is essential to the narrative is here. Lines that have found their way into the literature about the poem have been translated with an eye to the scholarly discussions that they have generated. Omissions can often be gleaned from the context and are, for the most part, trivial.

The notes to the text of this translation have been gathered with a eye to helping the reader understand either the context within which the action of the poem takes place or the artistic purpose of the author. Although both Latin editions were of value to me,[124] I have avoided the numerous classical references that would be useful mostly to the specialist. I have included quotations and epitomes from various sources.[125] There has been no attempt to reevaluate Frederick's first two Italian campaigns, but rather I tried to provide a background that will make the poem more pleasurable to the reader. I have not placed numbers that refer to notes in the text, because I believe that *Barbarossa in Italy* largely stands on its own as a well-told, intelligible story, and because they would pose a threat of breaking the continuity and thus flattening the verse.

Wayne State University

NOTES TO INTRODUCTION

1. For more information on this period, see Geoffrey Barraclough, *The Origins of Modern Germany* (Oxford: Basil Blackwell, 1947); idem, *The Medieval Papacy* (London: Thames & Hudson, 1968); Ute-Renate Blumenthal, *The Investiture Controversy. Church and Monarchy from the Ninth to the Twelfth Century* (Philadelphia: University of Pennsylvania Press, 1988); Horst

Fuhrmann, *Germany in the High Middle Ages, 1050-1200,* trans. Timothy Reuter (Cambridge: Cambridge University Press, 1986); Karl Hampe, *Germany under the Salian and Hohenstaufen Emperors,* trans. R. F. Bennett (Totowa, NJ: Rowan & Littlefield, 1973); Charles Homer Haskins, *The Renaissance of the Twelfth Century* (1927; reprint, Cambridge, MA: Harvard University Press, 1957); Alfred Haverkamp, *Medieval Germany 1056-1273* (Oxford: Oxford University Press, 1988); John Kenneth Hyde, *Society and Politics in Medieval Italy* (New York: St. Martin's, 1973); Karl Leyser, *Medieval Germany and its Neighbours, 900-1250* (London: Hambledon, 1982); Peter Munz, *Frederick Barbarossa. A Study in Medieval Politics* (Ithaca: Cornell University Press, 1969); Marcel Pacaut, *Frederick Barbarossa,* trans. A. J. Pomerans (New York: Charles Scribner, 1970); Timothy Reuter, *Germany in the Early Middle Ages, c. 800-1056* (London: Longman, 1991); Gerd Tellenbach, *Church, State and Christian Society at the Time of the Investiture Contest,* trans. and ed. R. F. Bennett (1959; reprint, New York: Harper & Row, 1970); Walter Ullmann, *A Short History of the Papacy in the Middle Ages* (London: Methuen, 1972); and Daniel Philip Waley, *The Italian City Republics,* 3d ed. (London: Longman, 1988).

2. Irene Schmale-Ott, ed., *Carmen de gestis Frederici I. imperatoris in Lombardia,* Monumenta Germaniae Historica. Scriptores rerum Germanicarum in usum scholarum, vol. 62 (Hanover: Hahn, 1965), p. xvi.

3. For the variety of opinion see Max Manitius, *Geschichte der lateinischen Literatur des Mittelalters* (1931; reprint, Munich: C. H. Beck'sche Verlags-buchhandlung, 1973), 3:687; Francesco Novati, *Le Origini,* vol. 2 of *Storia letteraria d'Italia,* continued and completed by Angelo Monteverdi (Milan: Vallardi, 1926), p. 601; Giovanni Pesanti, "Il 'Pergaminus,' Prolegomeni ad una edizione critica," *Bergomum* 7 (1913): 9-10. It is also implicit in Mazzi's theory. See Angelo Mazzi, *Note suburbane, con un' appendice sui mille homines Pergami del 1156* (Bergamo: Pagnoncelli, 1892),

pp. 17-18; F. J. E. Raby, *A History of Secular Latin Poetry in the Middle Ages* (Oxford: Clarendon Press, 1934), 2:160; and Schmale-Ott, pp. xvi-xvii.

4.   Eva Matthews Sanford, "The Twelfth Century. Renaissance or Proto-Renaissance?" *Speculum* 26 (1951): 638.

5.   Erwin Panofsky, *Renaissance and Renascences in Western Art* (1960; reprint, New York: Harper & Row, 1972), p. 84.

6.   A number of variations in spelling occur in a manner characteristic of that area. See Ernesto Monaci, ed., *Gesta di Federico I. in Italia*. Fonti per la Storia d'Italia, vol. 1 (Rome: Forzani, 1887), p. xxix. Also, although the codex has a modern binding, there is, among the remnants of an earlier one, a parchment document dating from 1309 by an imperial notary named Bernard Achiley. It confirmed a gift to the hospital of Borgo San Donnino, the modern Fidenza, a city about ten kilometers northwest of Parma. There is also a sixteenth-century gloss made by someone with a knowledge of Lombardy (Schmale-Ott, p. viii).

7.   Wilhelm von Giesebrecht, "Sopra il Poema recentemente scoperto intorno all' Imperatore Federico I. Lettera al Prof. Ernesto Monaci in Roma," *Archivio della Società Romana di Storia Patria* 3 (1880): 49-62 at p. 52; idem, "Neue Gedichte auf Kaiser Friedrich I.," *Sitzungsberichte der königlich bayerische Akademie der Wissenschaften. Historische Klasse* 2 (Dec. 6, 1874): 269-89 at p. 276.

8.   But Arsenio Frugoni, *Arnaldo da Brescia nelle fonti del secolo xii,* Istituto Storico Italiano per il Medio Evo, Studi Storici, 8-9 (Rome: ISIME, 1954), will go no further than to call him the anonymous Lombard.

9.   Jorg Jarnut, "Gli inizi del Commune in Italia. Il caso di Bergamo," *Archivio Storico Bergamasco* 3 (1983): 209.

10.   Wilhelm Gundlach, *Heldenlieder der deutschen Kaiserzeit* (Innsbruck: Wagner, 1899), 3:458.

11.   Antonio Pesenti, "La Chiesa nel primo periodo di vita communale," in Antonio Rimoldi, Adriano Caprioli, and Luciano Vaccaro, eds., *Diocesi di Bergamo* (Brescia: Editrice La Scuola,

1988), pp. 61-90. For more information on the internal conditions in Bergamo, which, I suspect, had an important influence on the creation of this poem, see Maria Luisa Scalvini, *Bergamo* (Bari: Laterza, 1987), pp. 25-30; Jorg Jarnut, "Gli inizi"; idem, *Bergamo, 568-1098. Verfassung-, sozial-, und Wirthschaftsgeschichte einer lombardischen Stadt im Mittelalter* (Wiesbaden: Steiner, 1979); C. Capasso, "Guelfi e Ghibellini a Bergamo," *Bergomum* 15,3 (1921): 1-44; Giovanni Cremaschi, *Mosè del Brolo e la cultura a Bergamo nei secoli xi e xii* (Bergamo: Società Editrice S. Alessandro, 1945); and Bortolo Belotti, *Storia di Bergamo e dei Bergamaschi,* 7 vols. (Bergamo: Poligrafiche Bolis, 1959).

12. Schmale-Ott, pp. xv-xvi.

13. Karl Wenck, "Thadeus de Roma," *Neues Archiv der Gesellschaft für ältere deutsche Geschichtskunde* 9 (1884): 202, 10 (1885): 170; and K. Pivec and H. Heimpel, "Neue Forschungen zu Dietrich von Niem," *Nachrichten der Akademie der Wissenschaften in Göttingen. Philologisch-Historische Klasse* 4 (1951): 23, 25.

14. For the varying opinions see Gundlach, 3:461-67; Henry Simonsfeld, *Jahrbücher des deutschen Reiches unter Friedrich I., 1152-1158* (1908; reprint, Berlin: Duncker & Humblot, 1967), p. 313 n. 112; and Schmale-Ott, pp. xiv-xv.

15. Mazzi, *Note suburbane*, pp. 377-82.

16. Belotti, 1:346. Cremaschi, *Mosè del Brolo*, p. 41; Monteverdi, pp. 598-99. Pesanti, pp. 3-4; Schmale-Ott, pp. xiii, xxiv. This misreading was noted by Luigi Chiodi, "Gli inizi del commune di Bergamo," *Bergomum*, n.s. 41 (1967): 1-29 at p. 27; and Giovanni Antonucci, "Magister Johannes Asinus de Gandino," *Bergomum*, n.s. 7 (1933): 218.

17. Giovanni Antonucci followed Johannes Asinus through the local documents and periodically published those that mentioned him. See "Un nuovo documento a Giovanni Asino," *Bergomum*, n.s. 9 (1935): 64-65; idem, "Documenti inediti su Giovanni Asino," *Bergomum*, n.s. 10 (1936): 41-45; and idem, "Magister Johannes Asinus, Documenti inediti," *Bergomum*, n.s. 12 (1938): 32-41.

18.   Giesebrecht, "La Lettera a Monaci," p. 56; idem, "Neue Gedichte," p. 280.

19.   J. Sturm, *Der Ligurinus. Ein deutsches Heldengedicht zum Lobe Kaiser Friedrich Rotbarts*, Studien und Darstellungen aus dem Gebiete der Geschichte, 8, 1 and 2 (Freiburg im Breisgau: Herder, 1911), p. 232.

20.   Damien van den Eynde, "Du nouveau sur deux maîtres lombards contemporains du Maître des Sentences," *Pier Lombardo* 2 (June, 1953): 6-8. Gerhoch's letter can be found in Migne, PL 193:489. Giovanni Cremaschi, "Nuovo contributo alla biografia di Mosè del Brolo," *Bergomum*, n.s. 28 (1954): 51-56.

21.   Haskins thought a great deal of him: "A Latin poet, a translator from the Greek, a grammarian and a collector of Greek manuscripts, he might almost hold his own three hundred years later. We cannot call him a humanist, for his culture reflects rather the theological preoccupations of his age, but he was at least a Hellenist and is entitled to an honorable place in conjunction with the Renaissance of the twelfth century." Charles Homer Haskins, "Moses of Bergamo," *Byzantinische Zeitschrift* 23 (1920): 142.

22.   Visconti's title for the Trivulzian manuscript, "The Deeds of Frederick Redbeard," shows his classical training. Nero's given name was Lucius Domitius Ahenobarbus. "The family of Domitii Ahenobarbi belonged to the Republican nobility. They could boast a line of consuls that extended back over two hundred years, while family legend traced their fame to the very infancy of the Roman Republic. Castor and Pollux, it was said, had foretold the Roman victory over the Latins at Lake Regillus to Lucius Domitius, providing proof of their divinity by stroking his cheeks and giving him the bronze beard that gave rise to the family's *nomen.*" Miriam T. Griffin, *Nero. The End of a Dynasty* (New Haven: Yale University Press, 1984), p. 20.

23.   Gundlach's title is translated: "The Story of the Conquest of Milan," which can be found in his anthology 3:380-467.

24. Robert Holtzmann, "Das Carmen de Frederico I. imperatore aus Bergamo und die Anfänge einer staufischen Hof-historiographie," *Neues Archiv der Gesellschaft für ältere deutsche Geschichtskunde* 44 (1922): 252-313.

25. Monaci believed that the manuscript was from the thirteenth or fourteenth century, but Schmale-Ott maintained that it dated from no later than the last third of the thirteenth century. Monaci, *Gesta di Federico I,* p. xxi; Schmale-Ott, p. viii.

26. This position was first articulated by Giesebrecht. Monaci (p. vii) agreed with him and added that the poet also spoke of the castle of Vigevano, another casualty of Frederick's Italian wars, as if it no longer existed (vv. 1727-28). But Schmale-Ott (pp. xviii-xix) is skeptical. If the poet wanted to be unambiguously clear about the destruction of Milan, she argued, he would have used the perfect tense *(urbs fuit)* not the imperfect *(urbs erat).* He had done precisely this in other similar cases. Giesebrecht's arguments on the time of the composition can be found on pages 53-54 of his Italian letter to Monaci and on pages 276-77 of his German article based upon the letter.

27. Gundlach discussed the time of composition on pages 459-61 of the third volume of his anthology.

28. Schmale-Ott, pp. ix-x. She found Giesebrecht's theory that relates the poem's unfinished state to a change in Bergamo's political orientation to be no more than a vague hypothesis. Could this change have been so rapid, she asked, to cause the poet to break off his work in the middle of a sentence? For her complete argument against Giesebrecht, see pp. xix-xx.

29. Schmale-Ott, p. x, n. 9.

30. Dietrich Becker, "Die Belagerung von Crema bei Rahewin, im *Ligurinus* und im *Carmen de gestis Frederici I. imperatoris in Lombardia*" (Ph.D. diss., Julius-Maximilian University at Würzburg, 1975), pp. 60-67.

31. There are, however, a number of mistakes. For example, when Frederick first descended from the Alps on his coronation visit, he

met Italian representatives at Roncaglia, not at Verona, as it was stated in the poem. Frederick granted rights of coinage to Cremona in 1155, not 1156. The poem also reports that Frederick was accompanied by 4,000 knights when he came to Italy, but we know from the emperor's letter to Otto that he only had 1,800. See also Schmale-Ott, pp. xxix-xxxii.

32. Schmale-Ott, pp. xxxii, xl. Gottfried Koch, *Auf dem Wege zum Sacrum Imperium. Studien zur ideologischen Herrschaftsbegründung der deutschen Zentralgewalt im 11. und 12. Jahrhundert,* Forschungen zur mittelalterlichen Geschichte 20 (Vienna: Hermann Böhlaus, 1972), p. 168, agreed with Giesebrecht that, in general, the poem confirms rather than expands our knowledge of the period; but Koch's study did not involve a detailed examination of the work.

33. In one of its most important passages, the poem alone relates the encounter of Frederick with the scholars of Bologna in 1155. The law that the emperor promulgated at the time conformed to the *Authentica Habita,* which Frederick had inserted into the *Corpus Iuris Civilis* at Roncaglia, dated November 1158. This privilege acknowledged for the first time the legal personality of a European university by recognizing the special position of the masters and the students in the commune.

34. Giesebrecht, "La Lettera a Monaci," p. 57; idem, "Neue Gedichte," p. 281.

35. Antonio Pagano, *Sul Poema Gesta di Federico I in Italia* (Naples: Gennaro & Morano, 1906), pp. 76-83.

36. Monteverdi, p. 600. On this point, Pagano (p. 75) quoted from one of Toracca's university lectures given in 1904: "The historical poems and versified chronicles have been considered as documents of history and culture; and this way of seeing them is not inexact but incomplete. It is necessary to consider these poems as historical sources in a larger sense, for they concern the life, the habits, the customs, and the traditions of the Italian people. They are documents of the state of its mind and of the sentiments

of the authors as well as their contemporaries. Only thus is it possible to recognize the complete importance of these compositions." (My translation.) Koch (pp. 168-69) echoed these ideas.

37. D. W. Robertson Jr., *A Preface to Chaucer. Studies in Medieval Perspectives* (Princeton: Princeton University Press, 1969), p. 164.

38. Schmale-Ott, pp. xlii-xlv. According to her, the poet saw Frederick more as a restorer of peace and order and less as a sovereign.

39. Pagano, p. 99.

40. Monteverdi, pp. 599-600.

41. Becker, p. 335.

42. Both Rahewin (3:46) and Gunther (8:98-168) gave this speech to Count Guido of Biandrate, an imperial partisan. Holtzmann, p. 293, considered it a mistake on the part of our poet to attribute it to a Milanese consul. But is it? Surely the point becomes stronger when the speech is delivered by one hostile to the emperor. Barbarossa laid great weight on the legality of his position. Heinrich Appelt, "Friedrich Barbarossa und die italienischen Kommunen," in *Friedrich Barbarossa,* ed. Gunther Wolf, *Wege der Forschung,* vol. 390 (Darmstadt: Wissenschaftliche Buchgesellschaft, 1975), p. 85. This is a reprint of the article, which originally appeared in vol. 72 of *Mitteilungen des Instituts für österreichische Geschichtsforschung* in 1964.

43. Ernst Robert Curtius, *European Literature and the Latin Middle Ages,* trans. Willard R. Trask (Princeton: Princeton University Press, 1953), p. 177. Curtius incorrectly stated that these lines were spoken of Frederick II.

44. Repeated twice, vv. 70, 664.

45. Giuseppe Chiri, *La poesia epico-storica latina dell'Italia medioevale,* Istituto di filologia romanza della R. Università di Roma, Studi e Testi (Modena: Società Tipografica Modense, 1939), p. 81.

46. Ibid., pp. 49-50.

47. Robertson, p. 170.

48. Frugoni, p. 93.

49. Ferdinand Gregorovius, *History of the City of Rome in the Middle Ages*, trans. Annie Hamilton (London: G. Bell & Sons, 1896), 4,2:546.

50. Frugoni, p. 95.

51. Usseglio wrote: "Among the contemporaries, one alone shows himself less severe on Arnold. He was the anonymous, probably a Bergamask, who wrote...." (My translation.) Leopoldo Usseglio, *I Marchesi di Monferrato in Italia ed in Oriente durante i secoli XII e XIII*, ed. Carlo Patrucco, 2 vols., XIX Congresso Storico Subalpino (Milan: Miglietta, 1926), 1:264. The poet told the story so well that Frugoni (p. 93) could not determine whether he was present, or whether he imaginatively recreated the event from what he had heard.

52. R. G. Collingwood, *The Idea of History* (1946; reprint, Oxford: Oxford University Press, 1980), p. 214. According to Schmale-Ott (pp. xxvi-xxvii), the poet always seemed to remain inside the event that he was narrating. Things were not always seen from the imperial perspective, and all major characters were allowed to step on stage and have their say.

53. Becker, p. 59. See also pp. 49-50.

54. Schmale-Ott, p. xxi.

55. Becker, pp. 330-35.

56. Cremaschi, *Mosè del Brolo*, p. 45; Monteverdi, p. 602.

57. Chiri, pp. 7-8, 59.

58. Monteverdi, pp. 602-3.

59. Monaci, *Gesta di Federico I*, p. x.

60. Haskins was also influenced by this bias. Although he did not mention this poem in his *Renaissance of the Twelfth Century*, its two sisters, the *Ligurinus* and the *Gesta Friderici* of Gottfried of Viterbo were considered as "far-off imitations of the ancients" (p. 274) and mere versified chronicles (p. 273), which were discussed in the chapter of history writing, not in the one on Latin poetry.

61. Monteverdi, p. 602.

62.   A discussion of techniques used by these poets can be found in Chiri, Chapter Four, "La Technica," pp. 59-80. Schmale-Ott also admired the poet's artistry: "Frequently changing scenes, backward glances, interpolation, allegorical personification help to prevent the monotony of the bare course of events and produce dramatic tension, which increased through the slow-moving episodes." (My translation.) Schmale-Ott, p. xxi.

63.   Gundlach, 3:450.

64.   "An epic is a poem including history," said a modern epic poet. Ezra Pound, "Date Line," in *Literary Essays,* ed. T. S. Eliot (London: Faber & Faber, 1954), p. 86.

65.   "Merely from the rhetorical character of medieval poetry, it follows that, in interpreting a poem, we must ask, not on what 'experience' it was based, but what theme the poet set himself to treat." Curtius, p. 158.

66.   Peter Dronke, *Poetic Individuality in the Middle Ages* (Oxford: Oxford University Press, 1970), p. 19.

67.   As Robert Graves said: "Wherever surviving records are meagre I have been obliged to fill in the gaps of the story with fiction, but have usually had an historical equivalent in mind: so that if exactly this or that did not happen, something similar probably did." Robert Graves, *Count Belisarius* (1938; reprint, New York: Penguin Books, 1954), p. 8. Frustrated by Lucan's unhistorical attitude, Macaulay wrote at the back of his volume of *The Civil War,* "...the furious partiality of Lucan takes away much of the pleasure which his talents would otherwise afford. A poet, who is, as has been often said, less a poet than a historian, should to a certain degree conform to the laws of history." Quoted in George Otto Trevelyan, *The Life and Letters of Lord Macaulay* (London: Longman, Green & Co., 1876), 1:459.

68.   Robert L. Benson, "Political *renovatio.* Two Models from Roman Antiquity," in *Renaissance and Renewal in the Twelfth Century,* ed. Robert L. Benson and Giles Constable (Cambridge, MA: Harvard University Press, 1982), pp. 339-86, at p. 379.

69. Becker, p. 311.

70. Schmale-Ott, p. xxiv; Becker, p. 28.

71. Gundlach, 3:451.

72. Otto, Bishop of Freising, and Rahewin, *The Deeds of Frederick Barbarossa*, trans. and ed. Charles C. Mierow with Richard Emery (New York: Columbia University Press, 1953), p. 177 (3:5), hereafter Mierow. Schmale-Ott (p. xxii) claimed this delay in Poland gave Milan time to overthrow Pavia, but this is not mentioned in the text (vv. 1615-1761).

73. Monaci, *Gesta di Federico I*, p. xi. Of Monaci's citations, Pagano counted 450 from Vergil, 60 from Lucan, 20 from Ovid, 18 from Statius, 3 from Horace and some from Propertius, Martial and Juvenal.

74. Karl Langosch, review of *Carmen de gestis Frederici I. imperatoris in Lombardia,* by Irene Schmale-Ott, in *Mittellateinisches Jahrbuch* 6 (1970): 293-95, at p. 295. Pagano stated that the imitation in this poem seemed to be made from memory (p. 37). The poet did not repeat mechanically but rethought and adapted what his memory suggested to him. Schmale-Ott claims the use of classical models as more than mere empty form but as fundamental to this poem, which wanted to raise Frederick to the level of an archetypal figure like Aeneas. Frederick is not called emperor a single time, and Schmale-Ott maintains that this was an attempt to follow Vergil's treatment of Aeneas. Schmale-Ott, pp. xxvii-xxviii.

75. According to Raby, 2:153, if Italian poets did not use the new rhythms that were being developed in the north, and if they adhered to classical forms, they felt no such attachment to ancient stories. "The eyes of men were fixed on present events. The life of the cities was both various and exciting; the poets themselves lived not in cloisters remote from world affairs, but in the very center of great happenings. Of what could they sing but of the history that was being made before their eyes?"

76. Kenneth Quinn, *Virgil's Aeneid. A Critical Description* (Ann Arbor: University of Michigan Press, 1968), pp. 31-38.

77. Pagano, p. 43.

78. Curtius, p. 105. In his foreword (p. ix), Curtius commented that: "In my book there will also be things which I could not have seen without C. G. Jung."

79. Pagano, p. 57.

80. Monteverdi, p. 602.

81. Curtius, pp. 162-65. Viscardi found this medieval version of the Judgment of Paris to be *naturale perfettamente* for the epoch. Antonio Viscardi, *Le Origini*, vol. 1 of *Storia letteraria d'Italia*, 4th ed. (Milan: Vallardi, 1966), p. 215.

82. Michael Alexander, *The Poetic Achievement of Ezra Pound* (Berkeley and Los Angeles: University of California Press, 1981), pp. 142-43.

83. Curtius, pp. 275-76.

84. "*Hyperbaton* (*transgressio, transcensio*) signifies a freer word order in which what belongs together grammatically is separated by intervening words." Also according to Curtius, pp. 274 and 285 n. 37, medieval mannerists took delight in dividing words in this way.

85. Gundlach, 3:449; Langosch, review of Schmale-Ott, p. 294.

86. Pagano, p. 70.

87. Manitius, p. 687; Raby, 2:159; and Langosch, *Die deutsche Literatur des lateinischen Mittelalters in ihrer geschichtlichen Entwicklung*, (Berlin: W. de Gruyter, 1964), p. 157; idem, review of Schmale-Ott, p. 297, all praised the quality of the verse.

88. The material for this section was taken from Holtzmann's article cited above (esp. 277-86; 308-10). Holtzmann may also have been influenced by Konrad Burdach, who argued that Walther von der Vogelweide incorporated terms from the imperial chancellery in his work and propagated the official position of Hohenstaufen imperial politics. Konrad Burdach, *Walther von der*

Vogelweide. Philologische und historische Forschungen (Leipzig: Duncker & Humblot, 1900).

89.   Walter Stach, "Politische Dichtung im Zeitalter Friedrichs I., Der *Ligurinus* im Widerstreit mit Otto und Rahewin," *Neue Jahrbücher für deutsche Wissenschaft* 13 (1937): 385-410. Idem, "*Salve, mundi domine!* Kommentierende Betrachtungen zum Kaiserhymnus des Archipoeta," *Berichte über die Verhandlungen der sächsischen Akademie der Wissenschaften zu Leipzig. Philologisch-Historische Klasse* 91,3 (1939): 5-58.

90.   Stach, "Politische Dichtung," p. 388. For Stach, under the metaphysical surface of the text ran the swift current of *Realpolitik*.

91.   For example, Stach believed that the use of the slogan, *prima Francia*, by Gunther and others as a synonym for the empire was meant to counteract the imperial pretensions of France among other things.

92.   E. Ottmar, "Das Carmen de Friderico I. Imperatore aus Bergamo und seine Beziehungen zu Otto-Rahewins *Gesta Friderici*, Gunthers *Ligurinus* und Burchard von Ursbergs *Chronik*," *Neues Archiv der Gesellschaft für ältere deutsche Geschichtskunde* 46 (1926): 430-89.

93.   Franz-Josef Schmale, Introduction to the *Gesta Frederici seu rectius cronica*, by Otto of Freising and Rahewin, Ausgewählte Quellen zur deutschen Geschichte des Mittelalters, vol. 17 (Berlin: Deutscher Verlag der Wissenschaften, 1965), pp. 48-58.

94.   Schmale also believed that the poet of the *Ligurinus* knew *Barbarossa in Italy*, since nothing speaks against the possibility that the poem was completed and given to the emperor (p. 54), and that it showed startling agreements with the *Chronicle* of Burchard of Ursberg (p. 55).

95.   Langosch, *Deutsche Literatur*, pp. 149-52. Langosch first gave his views on this topic in *Politische Dichtung um Friedrich Barbarossa* (Berlin, 1943).

96.   Fuhrmann, English ed., p. 153. I believe that Reuter's translation is from the second edition, which appeared in 1983.

97. For further discussion of this problem see Munz, pp. 125-40; Schmale-Ott, pp. xl-xlv; Becker, pp. 342-49; and Thomas Szabo, "Herrscherbild und Reichsgedanke: Eine Studie zur höfischen Geschichtsschreibung unter Friedrich Barbarossa" (Ph.D. diss., Albert-Ludwig University at Freiburg, 1971). See also Koch, pp. 165-69; Joachim Bumke, *Mäzene im Mittelalter, Die Gönner und Auftraggeber der höfischen Literatur in Deutschland 1150-1300* (Munich: C. H. Beck'sche Verlags-buchhandlung, 1979), pp. 151 and 374 n. 461; Peter Ganz, "Friedrich Barbarossa. Hof und Kultur," in Alfred Haverkamp, ed., *Friedrich Barbarossa. Handlungsspielräume und Wirkungsweisen des staufischen Kaisers* (Sigmaringen: Jan Thorbecke, 1992), pp. 623-50; Peter Johanek, "Kultur und Bildung im Umkreis Friedrich Barbarossas," in Haverkamp, ed., *Friedrich Barbarossa,* pp. 651-78; Rüdiger Schnell, ed., *Die Reichsidee in der deutschen Dichtung des Mittelalters,* Wege der Forschung, vol. 589 (Darmstadt: Wissenschaftliche Buchgesellschaft, 1983), pp. 4-13; and Erwin Assmann, ed., Gunther, *Ligurinus,* Monumenta Germaniae Historica. Scriptores rerum Germanicarum in usum scholarum, vol. 63 (Hanover: Hahn, 1987), pp. 111-12.

98. Stach, *Politische Dichtung,* p. 406.

99. Ibid., p. 403 (my translation). This quotation is Stach's interpretation of *Ligurinus* 3:576ff., but Stach identified the Barbarossa of Gunther with the historical Barbarossa.

100. Tellenbach, p. 115.

101. Fuhrmann, English ed., p. 71.

102. Albert Brackmann, "The Beginnings of the National State in Medieval Germany and the Norman Monarchies," in *Medieval Germany 911-1250. Essays by German Historians,* trans. and ed. Geoffrey Barraclough (New York: Barnes & Noble, 1938), 2:289.

103. Walter Bulst, "Politische und Hofdichtung der Deutschen bis zum hohen Mittelalter," *Deutsche Vierteljahrsschrift für Literaturwissenschaft und Geistesgeschichte* 15 (1937): 194.

104. Fuhrmann, English ed., p. 71.

105. Turoldus, *The Song of Roland. An Analytical Edition*, trans. Gerard Brault (University Park: Pennsylvania State University Press, 1978), 2:198-200, 2322-34.

106. Marc Bloch, *Feudal Society*, trans. L. A. Manyon (Chicago: University of Chicago Press, 1964), p. 100. It is not surprising that Curtius found epideictic oration to have a strong influence on medieval poetry, since its principal topic was eulogy. Italy seemed especially open to this type of literature. "Properly enough it is to Italy, where alone the Roman tradition of urban life survived all through the Middle Ages, that we owe a number of such panegyrical poems, some of which must be reckoned among the pearls of medieval poetry." Curtius, pp. 155, 157.

107. Holtzmann, p. 311 (my translation).

108. Mierow, p. 170.

109. Becker, p. 342 n. 1.

110. Holtzmann, p. 310. Holtzmann used the term *Mäzen*, (patron, literally Maecenas) to refer to Frederick, but the inference is the same. "Rainald, who was educated at the advanced schools of Hildesheim and Paris, was certainly the man to awaken in the emperor a realization of the significance of scholarship and the double wish: to be its patron and through it to be celebrated himself." (My translation.)

111. Holtzmann, 284; Langosch, *Deutsche Literatur*, p. 152.

112. Mierow, p. 159 (2:41). For a fuller treatment of Otto's view of history, see Walter Lammers, "Weltgeschichte und Zeitgeschichte bei Otto von Freising," in *Die Zeit der Staufer: Geschichte-Kunst-Kultur*, vol. 5, ed. Reiner Haussherr (Stuttgart: Würtembergisches Landesmuseum, 1977), pp. 77-90.

113. Ibid, pp. 287-88 (4:59).

114. On this point see J. B. Gillingham, "Why Did Rahewin Stop Writing the *Gesta Frederici?*" *English Historical Review* 83 (1968): 294-303. See also Holtzmann, pp. 287-88.

115. In speaking of medieval historiography, Marc Bloch stated (p. 90): "The criticism of evidence, almost inseparable from any form of study, was certainly not absolutely unknown – as is proved by the curious treatise of Guibert de Nogent on relics. But no one dreamed of applying it systematically to ancient documents – not, at least, before Abelard; and even with this great man it was still rather restricted in scope. A bias towards the rhetorical and heroic – the unfortunate legacy of classical historiography – weighed heavily on these writers. If certain monastic chronicles abound in records, the reason is that almost their sole purpose was the modest one of justifying the right of the community to its possessions. A Gilles d'Orval, on the other hand, in a work written in a loftier strain, dedicates himself to the task of recounting the great deeds of the bishops of Liège, and when by chance he comes across one of the first charters of urban liberties, that of the town of Huy, he declines to give an analysis of it, for fear it should weary his readers."

116. The account of Monaci's discovery of the manuscript and the story of its identification is contained in Ernesto Monaci, "Il Barbarossa e Arnaldo da Brescia in Roma," *Archivio della Società Romana di Storia Patria* 1 (1878): 459-65. Monaci also published a section on the siege of Milan (vv. 2194-2567). It is simply an extract from the complete edition, which was soon to appear, and it contained no introduction. Ernesto Monaci, *L'Assedio di Milano nel MCLVIII secondo l'anonimo di Cod. Vat. Ottob. 1463* (Rome, 1886).

117. Pesanti, p. 7; S. T. Collins, "*De gestorum Frederici I* Codice Vaticano," *Annali della Scuola Normale Superiore di Pisa*, ser. 2, 20 (1951): 98-103.

118. See n. 2 above.

119. Langosch, review of Schmale-Ott, pp. 293-95.

120. J. B. Hall, "The 'Carmen de gestis Frederici imperatoris in Lombardia,'" *Studi Medievali,* ser. 3, 26 (1985): 969-76.

121. Mierow, p. 11.

122. Although this is the first complete English translation, there is a small section on the death of Arnold of Brescia in English

prose in Ugo Balzani, *Early Chroniclers of Europe. Italy* (London: Society for Promoting Christian Knowledge, 1883), pp. 259-60. F. Querenghi translated the complete work into Italian prose in *Gesta di Federico I Barbarossa in Italia* (Bergamo, 1936). The text was extracted from *Bergomum* 8 & 9 for 1934 and 1935. A section of this poem can be found in Gundlach's anthology (3:383-423). Wilhelm von Giesebrecht, *Geschichte der deutschen Kaiserzeit,* 4th ed. 5 vols. in 6 (Braunschweig: C. A. Schwetschke und Sohn, 1875-81), 5:64-65 contains several pages about Frederick's meeting with the scholars at Bologna that are based quite closely on the poem.

123. Fenollosa in Hugh Kenner, *The Pound Era* (Berkeley and Los Angeles: University of California Press, 1971), p. 198.

124. The majority of notes without reference have been taken from those that Schmale-Ott provided for her edition.

125. Among those I have used are Oswald Holder-Egger, ed., *Gesta Federici I. Imperatoris in Lombardia auctore cive Mediolanensi,* Monumenta Germaniae Historica. Scriptores rerum Germanicarum, vol. 27 (Hanover: Hahn, 1892); Otto Morena, *Das Geschichtswerk des Otto Morena und seiner Fortsetzer über die Taten Friedrichs I in der Lombardei,* ed. F. Güterbock, Monumenta Germaniae Historica. Scriptores rerum Germanicarum, n.s. 7 (Berlin: Weidmann, 1930); Giovanni B. Testa, *History of the War of Frederick I against the Communes of Lombardy* (London: Smith, Elder, 1877); Giesebrecht, *Kaiserzeit*; and W. F. Butler, *The Lombard Communes* (1906; reprint, New York: Haskell House, 1969).

BARBAROSSA

IN ITALY

INVOCATION

MY MIND RECALLS so much. O muses grant
My prayer, and You, great King of Kings, give aid.
For nothing can begin well without You.
I try things that are worthy of this prince,
Whose presence will give strength to my attempt.   5

BOOK ONE

THERE WAS A CITY famous for its wars.
A lovely city, powerful and rich,
Liguria's capital, it was called Milan.
Her large population burned with love for Mars
And swaggered in the glory of its town.   10
To consuls, chosen by them every year,
They promised to control the way they lived,
And under these they kept the laws and faith.
Yet sharply they harassed the nearby towns
By pressing them for booty and with war,   15
And two captured cities were reduced to ruins.
First Lodi and then later Como fell.
They compelled obedience from wretched serfs
And heavily oppressed the conquered people,
Who were forbidden to repair their homes.   20
The rest of Liguria would be conquered next
Because their love for power was so great.
And who can count the tribute and the plunder,
The robberies or the castles smashed to ruins?
Who is able to relate the captives' pain,   25

1

Their chains, or their innumerable complaints?
The burghers, peasants, and the men who held
The citadels and sloping hills were frightened.
Not otherwise the herd flees through the woods
The lion and his quickly moving jaws.   30
There were no people who would dare begin
An open war against Milan. For fear
Had conquered all, and victory made her bold.
The furies and the passion to do harm
Inflamed the spirits of the nearby towns,   35
And those who ought to give each other help
Preferred to start an internecine war.
Wild Brescia bit Bergamo; Piacenza
And Cremona struck at Parma. Mantua
Was fearful of Verona, and Tortona   40
Of Pavia, and Pavia of Milan.
Since the rule of law was broken, all bore arms,
And the local cities ripped each other's throats.
With their minds corrupted people went insane,
Nor could the fear of God or the restraint   45
Of law prevent the oppression of the weak.
Just so the horse that feels himself more able
Wants to dominate the grassy meadow.
He neighs and he attacks, now here now there,
To wound his rivals with his hoofs or teeth.   50
Without protection no poor man was safe,
Nor were travelers secure from all the thieves.
Fraud, robbery, and deceit reigned everywhere.
Such was the state of Italy and Liguria.

DUKE FREDERICK then took up the reins of
    power,   55
Elected by the nod of kindly heaven.
He was pious and unequaled as a soldier
And descended from an ancient line of kings.
A wondrous legacy of strength and wisdom
Was biform nature's double gift to him.   60
Since his ears, as I have heard, were filled with
    rumors
And complaints that came from here and there,
He grieved and vowed to end the many evils.
So did our grieving Lord look on a world
Diseased with sin and drown by flood those men 65
Who had refused to take his healing grace.
It was the custom of the German kings
To go to Rome to take the crown, since none
Of them possessed the great imperial name,
Till consecrated hands had offered it.   70
Desiring to respect this custom, Frederick
Moved to go where the high priest held the crown.
But first he wished to see those hard Ligurians,
And find if evil reigned, as he had heard.
It was the season when the glaring sun   75
Will quickly melt the gray and frosty fields.
Then Frederick took the road and with him rode
An army of four times a thousand knights.
All magnates who resided in Liguria
Ran to meet the king when he descended.   80
Verona, in your fields they showed themselves
Prepared to serve their lord, who now approached.
Lodi and Como both were present there,

And many others who complained about
Their lot and charged Milan with serious crimes.   85
They lamented their expulsion from their homes
And their long oppression under brutal force.
Two cities had been lawlessly destroyed,
While they themselves had suffered war and rapine;
And thus they begged the mighty king's protection. 90
The rulers of Milan were also there,
And they excused themselves of all that blame,
One of them arose and spoke to Frederick:
"Great lord of kings, protector of the law,
Hail, king of Rome! Indeed you are most worthy.   95
Our citizens salute our lord and king,
And they rejoice to serve at your arrival.
Our people have been faithful to the crown
And always loved the honor of the realm.
Our purpose hasn't wandered. Use our men
   and gold,   100
Since we have a great abundance of them both.
The power of Milan exists to serve you.
No city is more loyal to the king
Or better or more zealous of the right.
Yet, many are complaining of our actions,   105
Like men from Lodi, Como, and Novara.
So I will answer charges, if you want.
Indeed there was a neighbor to Milan
Named Lodi, whose great pride brought her to ruin.
For she who would destroy us was destroyed,   110
And shame it is, I say, to tell this story:
So violent and cruel were men from Lodi
That in our fathers' time they often took

Us captive when they found us on their road,
And often we returned home bruised and naked.   115
No one could travel safely through that land,
Unless he had procured a guardian.
And so we often sent a nuncio,
Who gently begged for them to stop. He asked
In peace for restitution of the spoils.   120
But their rulers and their wisemen always answered:
Their people were too many to be kept
With lock and key. Each must defend himself
Or travel with a bodyguard, who can
Provide protection from the fear of robbery.   125
They made no effort to return the spoils.
Often offended by such answers, we
Declared a war against those evil men
And prepared to avenge ourselves with arms.
So when it came to blows, our men rose up   130
From everywhere and drove them to their gates.
The city was encircled, but those safe
Within the walls poured out their threats and curses.
Yet their pride would finally earn what it deserved;
The city was destroyed since God forsook it.   135
But we gave the peasants life and their ancestral
Land, and we quickly made a bond of peace.
Next Como, which possessed a mountain and
A nearby lake, began to beat and rob
Our citizens just like the men from Lodi.   140
Since we preferred to move towards peace not war,
We often asked those men to stop their crimes
And desist in bringing great disgrace to us.
For if our merchants took their wares to Como

And went there with a zeal for making gain,   145
They often came back destitute and naked;
And when they tried to trade for what they wanted,
Anyone could stop them on a whim.
For many years, O gracious lord, we bore
Such grievous insults, till the power of God   150
Had thrown them down and placed them in
     our hands.
Yet all citizens have been protected by us,
And we do not oppress those we have conquered,
But we forbid them to repair their cities.
We know, O pious king, if we permit   155
New walls, they will be followed by new wars.
For we are not the first to take up arms,
Nor first to move toward war. Desiring peace,
We never were the cause of such great evils.
We do not strike unless we have been struck,   160
And we will bother no one without reason.
Struck first, we conquered Lodi and then Como.
Struck first, we vexed Novara and Pavia.
Most excellent of kings, let us implore you,
Be gentle to the people of Milan.
Please be a generous leader and be kind   165
To us, as other kings who passed before.
We are prepared to serve you, where we can."
The monarch smiled and gave to them this answer:
"This discord weighs upon the royal mind.   170
Now if your people want to keep the peace,
My trust, my orders, and uphold the law,
They will be able to preserve my love.
But if you choose to live by twisted values

And lawlessly attack those living near, 175
Our might will not endure it. Magnates, swear
To keep our trust and to obey the law.
Convince the lesser folk to do the same."
They swore the oath as Frederick had commanded.
Afterwards, when a consul had returned, 180
He openly proclaimed the royal edict
To Milan, which rushed to send expensive gifts,
Temptations for the king to change his mind.
She hoped he would not bother with complaints
From the oppressed, or force her to desist; 185
So she could dominate as in the past.
But pious Frederick spurned her gifts and said:
"We will not take the things your city offers,
And we will not give our thanks, you may be sure,
Until by serving our decrees, you fear 190
The law and keep the peace with nearby towns.
You will retain our love by such behavior."
He then broke camp and went to see Liguria,
But he never housed his men within their cities.
From every town the loyal people ran 195
To bring him gifts and guide him through their
   land.
They showed him rivers and places right for camp.
This famous leader counseled them to love
The good of peace and follow righteousness.
Like a father speaking to his wayward sons, 200
He advised them to correct their way of life.
The Milanese who rode with him confessed
Their willingness to serve in words not deeds
And tried to change his mind with flattery.

The noble prince reproached them as a friend   205
And urged them to submit to his commands.
He asked if they would lead him through their land.

THERE IS a place not far from great Milan
To which the ancients gave the name of Moitia,
And there the church of John the Baptist stands.   210
They say it was established by her kings,
Whose lofty power filled it full of treasure.
The Roman princes on their way to Rome
By custom always stopped to pay a visit
And take the crown of the Ligurian kings.   215
Since Frederick wished to keep this ancient custom,
He requested that the Milanese
Allow their well-born men to guide him there.
The consul said to him: "Great king, we are
Prepared to do your will as best we can.   220
For we are bound by the chains of an oath.
But we fear our youth may be too bold
And may attack your knights. O greatest father,
They brood because you spurned our gifts and wish
To change the honors that we once enjoyed.   225
We dare not lead you safely to that place,
Unless you wish to go with just a few.
But if your pious grace is given to us,
And if you have the will to come with peace
That would not stain our city's ancient honor,   230
We'll lead you to the shrine of John the Baptist
Or wherever in our land you wished to go.
Our town will celebrate a splendid feast
With oaths of loyalty and lavish gifts."
The pious king had listened to this speech,   235

And now it was apparent that Milan
Refused to bow her neck before his yoke,
Unless he let her dominate, and smash
The towns, and subjugate as in the past.
Recalling the complaints of those she injured,   240
He kept his temper in control, because
He lacked the men to stop Milan by force.
And the former capital, Rome, still beckoned him
To come and take the sacred diadem.
He spoke: "Why have the people of Milan   245
So often tried to twist what I have said?
Do you suppose to win us with your gifts?
I said what I have said. I do not move.
I take no gifts, unless your people swear
To keep the peace and to obey our laws.   250
We turn away from proud and evil men
But show our grace to those who serve the right."
Then Frederick asked his magnates for advice;
He was uncertain whether he should seek
The church of John the Baptist, since Milan   255
Refused to lead him there with bands of knights.
The magnates urged the king to follow where
The rulers of Milan might wish to take him.
Before them they would fly the royal standard
So that no chance for trouble could arise.   260
The gracious leader took his men's advice
And gave his banners to the Milanese,
Who'd show the way and places right for camp.
Then with a kindly face he promised love.
But in hope of sparing their estates, they led   265
The royal army through deserted places

Where nothing else but water could be found,
And the barren land contained no food for mounts.
The customary market was not offered.
Thus the royal anger ordered men to take   270
Three wealthy castles named Rosate, Trecas,
And Galeate, which were soon despoiled,
And they destroyed a bridge on the Ticino
By which armed Milanese did usually
Attack the people on the other side.   275
These deeds disturbed Milan, whose citizens
Now spoke about the king without respect
And wanted, if they could, to do him harm.
But Frederick and his men had quickly crossed
The border of Milan at the Ticino   280
To see the other peoples of Liguria.

WITH MINDLESS RAGE Tortona and Pavia
Were equals in their mutual disgust,
But Tortona had an ally in Milan.
Although the king had hoped to end the struggle   285
Pavia was the only one who listened,
And this caused Frederick quite a bit of anguish.
He saw it might delay his trip to Rome,
The thing on which he doted. There he would join
The name of king to the imperial title.   290
But first it pleased him to reduce by siege
That ally of Milan, the proud Tortona.
So he called his knights together and he spoke:
"They spurn me in my kingdom. Look, my heroes,
My authority and power are ignored.   295
If small Tortona scorns my will, what will
The great cities and mighty peoples do?

10

Only a few will honor our decrees,
Unless Tortona is subdued by us and made
To pay the debt her wicked deeds have earned.   300
Perhaps our duty calls us to that course,
But however much we yearn for Rome, we still
Have time enough to bring Tortona down."
The knights gave their assent to his decision,
And toward the lofty city Frederick turned.   305
He saw Tortona's gates were closed to him,
And many men were manning her defenses.
Then he encircled the mountain and besieged
The town, which sat upon a fair-sized ridge.
When bold Milan had learned this, she became   310
Indignant, as when first her gifts were spurned
And castles useful to her were subdued;
She was indignant, since he had destroyed
A bridge and wished to break by siege a city
To which Milan had always given aid.   315
It was urged in an assembly that the consuls
Resign their ancient office, as is custom.
So from those who swore an oath before the king
They quickly took away the highest honor,
As it was wrong to serve a kindly lord,   320
And gave to men who did not fear to scorn
His laws the legal right to their submission.
On their advice they rushed to send two cohorts
Of cavalry and foot to help Tortona
And guard those friendly people from the king.   325
How ignorant is man of what must be.
How badly he foresees his disappointments.
The chosen quickly went, and as they left

A consul spoke a few words to arouse them:
"Now go brave men with bodies ripe for war.   330
Now go! The times demand we show our trust
To friends and give our usual help to those
Who stand exhausted and in great distress.
These people have remembered what they promised
And gave their help to allies and to friends.   335
King Frederick strives to take a loyal city,
And if the price is right, we'll all be next.
But if your strength protects our friend, Tortona,
Great glory and eternal fame will follow.
My men, I pray, now show your manly strength."   340
After the speech they hastened to that town,
Where in three days they happily arrived.
Tortona joyfully received these men,
And those enclosed within the city's ramparts,
Who only thought at first of where to hide,   345
Were now prepared to fight. So bold young men
Broke quickly from their gates to rob the few
That strayed about and threaten Frederick's camp.
The royal knights, aroused and quick to arm,
Rushed out and chased the enemy, who showed   350
His back as he fled up the mountain heights.
Just so a group of shepherds is accustomed
To keep rapacious wolves from sheep. They shout
At those who dare attack and follow them
To Alpine paths, relaxing when they lose them.   355
How often did Tortona dare descend
The mountain and invade the royal camp.
Following quickly after them, the knights
Rose up to press and strike the enemy,

Who sought refuge by fleeing up the hill.   360
The king had often asked them to use reason,
But his promise to forgive them went unheard
By people trusting blindly in Milan.
Rejecting peace and pardon, they scorned the king.
Thus desiring to defeat that haughty city,   365
Courageous Frederick built machines of war.
Machines to destroy the towers and the walls;
Machines to repel defenders from the ramparts;
Machines to subjugate that proud Tortona.
A ram and catapults were soon constructed.   370
Now watch the missiles break the walls apart
And shatter houses, while frightened peasants run.
Great stones flew through the middle of the city,
While spears launched from machines were
      killing men
And knocking youths prepared for battle from   375
The ramparts. A ram, suspended to increase
Its impact, smashed the thick joints of the walls.
But above the flames and fragments of their
      buildings,
The fields of spikes and the crashing of the ram,
Tortona fought in defense of her home.   380
A lofty tower, made of ancient stone,
Protected the area by the outer gate.
The Red Tower was the name they gave to it.
King Frederick took it with great force, and more
And more he terrified his weary foes.   385
Now people saw they could not hold the city,
And courage will fail with everything in ruins.
Whoever had rejoiced before with cheers

And games concealed the sorrow in his heart.
Regretting their aggression and their scorn   390
For royal mandates, now they asked for terms
And wanted to surrender, if the crowd
Of fearful Milanese did not forbid it.
Besides the war, drought and disease oppressed them,
And many died within the guarded walls.   395
The wells and fountains all were dry. Although
Grains were abundant, drinks were not. In vain
They hoped for rain, because the crescent moon,
Diana's slender horn, excluded hope.
It's much the same in burning Libya   400
When Phoebus drives the sun high in the sky.
Defeated by the war, disease and thirst,
They asked their clergy to appear before
The king and beg forgiveness, if they could.
Entering Frederick's camp with rapid steps,   405
They gave their trust and tearfully confessed:
"O pious king, the Heavens honor you
And want your reign to spread to many cities.
O father, look upon us with a smile.
Remember fortune changes; so don't despise   410
Our tears. Behold us lying at your feet,
Who humbly ask for safety and forgiveness.
Have mercy on us, ruler. Hear our prayers.
Because we boldly took up arms against you
And stupidly brought down your wrath upon us,   415
In sorrow now we want to pay the price.
To you belongs the city we so badly
Defended. Have your wish. Destroy our walls,
But let us and our allies go in freedom.

But if by chance you want to make us captives   420
And take what we possess, we would prefer
To suffer as we have, or even more.
Perhaps to die." The pious king replied:
"Too late you seek forgiveness, and too late
Your conquered people demand a victor's right.   425
Behold, we have besieged you for three months,
Speaking always of forgiveness and a truce,
But reckless and prepared for horrid battles,
You despised the peace we offered until now.
By trusting in your ramparts, you provoked us,   430
And now unable to resist, you seek
Our pardon. You have lost your minds indeed,
You who thought your walls could bring you victory.
In fact our reign would be forever shamed,
If small cities could despise us without risk.   435
Yet, take the freedom sought by your contrition.
The women, children, men, both young and old,
Are pardoned and can leave. But we will ruin
The city and the ruins will teach a lesson
So that others may fear to scorn the king.   440
Thus fortune varies. Thus the high and low
Will change their places when she spins her wheel."
So spoke the king, who then commanded that
No one should harm the refugees. Now watch
Those pardoned run from their ancestral homes,   445
As if their roofs were licked by hungry flames,
Or an earthquake crushed them, shaking them
   to ruins.
When the wretched people and their allies left,
The royal soldier ruled the captive city.

Now walls and towers crash into the dust;   450
Now Tortona falls to Frederick's anger.

THUS THE VICTOR could continue on his way
To Rome. But first he urged Liguria to love
The laws of peace and to reject harsh war,
And their best soldiers rode along with him.   455
On the Reno, where bright Bologna shines,
He camped and took a few days to revive
And restore his tired army's broken strength.
The people came there anxious to serve him.
These subjects of the just and prudent Guido   460
Were running out to meet him with their gifts
And also gave a great deal to his troops.
The professors and their students both approached,
And they all wished to see the Roman king.
Bologna, you produce so many scholars   465
Who labor day and night in different fields.
King Frederick was delighted to greet them,
And he spoke kindly, asking many questions:
What are the things that keep you in Bologna?
Why did you choose this place above the rest?   470
What burdens on you have the townsfolk laid,
And can they keep the promises they made?
Do they observe the rules for foreign guests?
A scholar with ability to answer
Spoke of their happy life and how they lived.   475
He said: "Great king, this land that we inhabit
Is filled with what is useful for a scholar.
Our students, who are eager and select,
Have come from every corner of the world,

And we are rich and bring you gold and garments.   480
In the middle of the city we rent houses
And fairly purchase goods that we all use,
Except for water, which is held in common.
Both day and night we concentrate and study,
And the time we spend here makes our labor
    sweet.   485
The people of this town give us much honor,
But we are sometimes bothered by one thing:
We are compelled to pay without discussion
A security for debts we do not owe,
Because they seek from us, who are not bound   490
By force of law, the debts owed by our neighbors.
Father, we beg, correct this evil custom.
Give your protection to our academics."
The king then asked the princes for advice
And made a law to give the scholars help.   495
No one who wished to study could be stopped
(Either in town or while he was in transit),
Because he had refused to pay a debt
For which there was no legal obligation.
The king requested that the citizens   500
Respect the scholars and their rights as guests.
In several days his men regained their strength,
And Frederick moved his camp to Tuscany.

MEANWHILE a messenger came to Milan,
Who told them of Tortona's fallen towers   505
And of the many evils they had suffered
Before surrendering to the warrior king.
The city was preoccupied with grief,

As if an evil herald told the fathers
About their sons, who cut the deep in ships,   510
That foreign people killed or captured them.
Then fathers, brides, and little grandsons cry.
Not otherwise did grief consume Milan,
Whose people raged and groaned at the misfortune.
Thus goaded by these thoughts that were so
   painful,   515
The magnates and plebeians quickly gathered
To find some comfort for their bitter lot.
When the murmurs had at last begun to quiet,
A consul rose and calmly spoke these words:
"O people, brilliant in the arts of war,   520
Whose reputation spreads throughout the world,
You're right to be disturbed by this injustice,
But do not be content with indignation.
Take courage and remember your fathers.
Recall the glory that cost a sea of blood   525
Our fathers had more often suffered hardships,
But a strong man's virtue conquers every foe.
Tortona, which had trusted in our help,
Has lost her walls. But we could use our wealth
To build them others. If we wished, we could   530
Replace their houses and restore those ramparts
That odious Pavia found so hateful
And that have often cost us so much work.
So then, my countrymen, raise up your spirit.
The times demand we spend the wealth we saved.   535
I pray that we will use our fathers' strength
To crush our foes and serve the ancient honor.
Pavia might be willing to resist us

To prevent Tortona rising as before,
But if they start a reckless war against us,   540
They'll find we have regained our strength and
   more."
All wanted to approve him when he finished,
And raised their hands and many times repeated
A mighty cry that climbed unto the sky.
The cohorts showed that they were in agreement   545
And joined the clamor, prompted by their leaders.
Once the consul saw he had approval,
He sent a legion to rebuild the walls
And to restore Tortona. So those friendly
People, forced to leave because of war,   550
Might return to where their fathers once had
   dwelled.
The troops with their provisions soon departed.
Through Piacenza they were given passage,
For Pavia had closed her borders to them,
Although the shortest route went through her
   lands.   555
And even citizens who feared the king
Agreed to yield and give a thousand thank-you's
To Milan for granting them so fine a gift.
Together they rebuilt Tortona's ramparts
And made the city better than it was.   560
Eagerly the legion and the peasants worked.
Some rebuilt the citadel and some the walls.
Some constructed homes, while others rolled large
   stones.
Now watch them joyfully take up their work,
Relieving others who, once battle lines   565

Are drawn, can hastily repel the foe.
The bees in summer flowers work no harder,
Who lead forth offspring once they are mature,
While others pack the honeycombs with honey
And gorge the cells with sweet and wondrous
    nectar.   570
Some give relief to those who are fatigued,
While others keep the drones far from the hive.
So too did the Ligurians, wanting to
Repair the city, rush to lend their help.
With sweat they raised the towers, walls, and
    ramparts.   575
Her enemy, Pavia, did not wish
Tortona to regain her former status
And caused her all the trouble that she could.
Yet often her aggressions boldly were
Repelled, and they finished what they had began.   580
Still in haste they sent a legate to Milan,
Who told her that Pavia moved towards war
And asked for help. A consul's speech aroused
The Milanese, who quickly took up arms
And in a frenzied state marched toward Pavia.   585
They built a wooden bridge with planks and beams,
Using not a little money and much work.
It was a marvelous bridge, which would allow
A thousand knights to cross together, and day
And night men stood in guard of it with arms.   590
When all were finally on the other side,
They devastated much within the region,
Burning, robbing, raping towns and villas.
Oppressing conquered peoples with large tributes,

This warlike race most bitterly attacked   595
Not only Lodi, Como, and Novara,
Who dared to bring complaints before the king,
But among their many robberies and aggressions,
The manors of the Bergamasks were taken,
And their wretched serfs were lawlessly
   despoiled.   600
And once Tortona's ramparts were repaired,
They still maintained their forces in that town
Until the walls had been completely strengthened.
For then the city could defend itself.
So troops from Milan were moving on the road   605
That ran across the lands of Piacenza.
Indeed the people of that town were bribed
To help the Milanese on this occasion.
This diminished the honor paid the king.

BOOK TWO

THE TRIP that Frederick started reached its end,   610
And having passed through many towns and
     nations,
He was rejoicing at the sight of Rome.
A legate of the Roman people ran
To meet him on the summit called Mount Joy,
And there Lord Frederick heard him make this
     speech: 615
"O king, let there be glory in your realm,
Life, honor, safety, and unbroken victory.
The Romans will exult at your arrival,
And eagerly we are prepared to serve you.
Yet we ask that you respect an old tradition,   620
For you must swear when you will pass our gates
To guard the city's honor and her pride
And rights demanded by the ancient senate.
Besides we seek the presents that you owe,
That kings when they first came have given us.   625
To enter Rome with joy you now must grant them.
Then happily we'll offer honors to you
And more devotion than you can remember."
Though Frederick was astonished by these words,
He answered briefly in a quiet voice: 630
"Let happiness remain in your possession.
Let fear and all adversity depart.
I do not come to stain your people's glory,
Nor does it please me to attack the senate.

22

I will return to home when I have taken   635
The sacred diadem, which custom grants me.
Yet I have never heard of that tradition
That you ask me to observe, nor will my knights
Allow me to swear the oath that you require.
But I will not forget if you obey me,   640
And I will repay you when the time is right."
Then Frederick and a host of his retainers
Proceeded to the city and approached
The gate it's said that Leo had constructed.
The senate, which had formerly been great,   645
And many citizens went out to meet him.
They claimed that Roman kings by ancient custom
Should swear an oath right there when they arrive
To take the sacred diadem in Rome.
But when the king dismissed them they retreated   650
And threatened that he made them now his foes.
Just so a beggar threatens and insults
If his request for money is denied.
But bitter words did not surprise the king,
Who passed the gate with all his men behind him   655
And boldly sought the temple of Saint Peter.
There sat the reverent Adrian as pope,
A man known for his character and learning.
According to the custom, he received
The monarch in the portal of the church   660
And led him in the building with great praise.
Then offering Mass, he placed the diadem
On his royal head with consecrated hands
And blessed him in the manner of a father.
The king displayed his presents at the altar,   665

Libations and rich gifts which he now offered
To thank the pope for praying for them all.
Moreover, when the holy Mass had ended,
He returned to camp with gladness in his heart
And the imperial title in his hands   670
To feast the soldiers at a lavish banquet.
The Roman people were enraged to fury.
With arms in hand they rushed from all directions
To occupy the district of Pope Leo,
Where, breaking locks, they vandalized the houses   675
And robbed supporters of the august king.
The clergy and the laity both suffered,
And even cardinals who remained nearby
After sacred rites had been concluded.
Now shouting and confusion filled the street,   680
And many fled in panic to the king,
Who camped nearby, next to the flowing Tiber.
When this report had come to royal ears,
The king commanded knights, who were not slow
To arm, to help those fleeing and despoiled.   685
And restrain Rome's reckless citizens by force.
The mounted knights then let their horses run,
And Frederick, armed and flushed for war, rode with
     them.
When the Roman phalanx saw the troops approach,
It was afraid and huddled in retreat.   690
But soon they struck their foes most violently.
It's as if a group of hunters sees two bears
Approach them from a distant mountain peak.
At first they're filled with terror at the sight,
But eager for a kill, they curb their fear   695

And chase the bears with hunting spears held tightly.
So did these greedy people rush to plunder,
And shouting, they engaged the knights in battle.
Some struggled hand to hand, while others shot
Their arrows at a distance or threw spears.   700
Most fiercely German knights and tough Ligurians
Rose up and forced the Romans to retreat.
The earth was strewn with weapons and the sound
Of shields and hollow helmets cracked the air.
Sublime on his high horse, observing all,   705
King Frederick rode around the battle line.
There was the young Duke Henry, bold and
    handsome.
Renowned was he, and dreadful was his sword.
He led a thousand knights, the very best,
Whom he encouraged by showing strength
    in battle.   710
What great confusion did he cause his foes!
Who could count the victors or the vanquished
Or tell the story of each single wound?
The bodies of the dead were everywhere,
And many horses fell struck through the chest.   715
Your handsome vigor cannot go unmentioned,
For, Manfred, you're the pride of all Liguria,
And the honor of your family honors you.
Your father Gozzo was both fierce and handsome,
A noble count just like his father Albert;   720
Their heir has not departed from their standards.
For no one in Liguria has a more
Attractive body or fights with greater skill.
He followed Frederick on his trip to Rome

And commanded troops of armed knights
    under him.   725
With them this man, who was renowned in battle,
Rushed like a lion to the middle of
The fray and struck those in his way with sword
And spear. The cohort with him fiercely raged
And pursued retreating foes just like their leader.   730
The Roman youths were driven toward the Tiber.
But they mustered and returned when they had
    learned
About their bitter loss and hard defeat.
They ran to bring their help from everywhere.
Again the battle raged, and both the armies   735
Wavered before the Romans fled once more.
Strong Germans and Ligurians pressed most fiercely,
And those they did not take or kill they scattered.
There is no doubt the victor, Frederick, ordered
His men to spare the vanquished as they fled.   740
Then he gave the signal to return, though few
Were lost and many prisoners were captured.
For now the horses of the sun had run
The course of day, and dewy night arose
To let those weary men restore their strength.   745
When morning chased the shadows from the earth,
The pope appeared and asked the king to do
As Mercy taught and give his captives to him.
The pontifex was honored by the monarch,
For gentle Frederick heard his prayers and freed   750
Those Romans whom he captured in the fight.
The king took up his tent and left the city,
Because he wished to see the countryside.

He wanted to bring down the Roman towers
That had been raised to guard the city's villas   755
And injure its opponents, if they wished.
Thus angered by the war, the king destroyed them
So that this haughty race might learn to fear
And to repent of that malicious battle.

THEN ARNOLD was residing in those regions,   760
Whom Brescia bore and honored overmuch.
His life was very hard and too austere;
He ate, but did not speak, with moderation.
A scholar with great confidence and knowledge,
He knew more than it was wise for him to know.   765
I judge that it will help your understanding
To speak about his end and what he believed:
He carped at common people and the priests,
Since he alone, he thought, lived morally,
And others were in error if they strayed   770
From what he taught. For nothing was above
Attack, not even actions of the pope.
He mixed the truth with falsity to please
The crowd. He damned the laymen who withheld
Their tithes as well as usury and war.   775
As Scripture teaches, he condemned luxury,
Dishonesty, and all the fleshly sins
That blocked the path to life. No vice was flattered.
But still he acted like a foolish doctor
Who amputates both hurt and healthy limbs,   780
And there were very few his wrath omitted.
He censured fallen priests and Simonists
Who thought to hold their office for a price.

He said the people ought not to confess
And never take the sacraments from them.   785
To him the monks who disobeyed their rule
Were not entitled to the name of monk.
Infatuated by the things that perish,
The popes, he said, have spurned a higher good.
They spend their time in selling court decisions   790
In disregard of all their other duties.
For this he judged they'd earn eternal death,
Since sinful men were bound, he claimed, by just
One rule: To love God and their neighbor not.
What evils flourish at the Roman See,   795
For popes, he said, had put a price on justice
And money had usurped the place of law.
From the head the evil flowed into the body
Of the Church, and every member yearned for rich
Rewards. So everything must have its price,   800
And what does not is held in great contempt.
This was the teaching of that famous Arnold
That pleased the masses by its novelty.
All Europe had been taken by this doctrine
Which first gathered bitter fruit in Italy.   805
O Brescia, you reflect your child's teaching,
Which had disturbed the peace of great Milan
And broke the easy faith of Rome's plebeians.
Wherever it was sown, it caused sedition,
Deceiving people in the guise of truth.   810
Although the pope desired to convert him,
His kind advice was never strong enough
To cause him to relinquish his beliefs.
In bitter language Arnold never stopped

Insulting the pope, nor would he quit his errors.   815
Frequent warnings often went astray,
And he rejoiced to see his fame increase.
Because his lying doctrines fooled the people,
The tearful pope desired to heal this sickness.
He found him worthy of anathema,   820
And hurled this doctor teaching schism from the
      Church,
So does the surgeon cut the rotting member
In order to protect the body's health.
But that did not restrain this master's tongue
From spreading his accustomed lies. He flayed   825
The church more harshly. Teaching as he taught,
He contradicted what the pope had sought.
Therefore he was reported and then jailed
By the Roman prefect acting for the king.
Then Frederick ordered him to judge this case,   830
And the learned doctor's doctrines were
      condemned.
So he discovered that he would suffer death
And fate had put a noose around his neck.
They asked him to reject his wicked theories
And be wise enough to make a full confession.   835
With confidence and courage that was astounding
He said his teachings seemed correct to him,
And he would not recant in face of death
Since nothing in them was absurd or harmful.
He sought a brief delay; he said he needed   840
Time to pray and tell his sins to Christ.
He bent his knees and raised his hands to heaven,
While sighs emerged from deep within his chest.

He spoke to God, but did not use his voice
To ask him to have mercy on his soul.   845
Then in a little while he stood prepared
To die, and the lictors looking on were moved
To tears by his display of piety.
Yet he was hanged, suspended by a rope.
It's said the king lamented, but too late.   850
What good was all your knowledge, learned
   Arnold?
What good your fasting and your discipline?
What good a life that is too strict and always
Spurns the easy path and carnal things?
O wretched man, what led you to attack   855
The church and brought you to this sorry rope?
Since that for which you suffered is condemned,
It will not quickly be restored to favor.
Your doctrines like yourself are turned to ashes,
And no relic may remain to honor you.   860

THE ROMAN towers ruined, the pious Frederick
Went to Albano where he made his camp.
A plague rose up and quickly gripped the troops.
Oppressive heat and heavy, noxious air
Infected many soldiers with a languor.   865
The thousands who were withered by a fever
Were also struck by violent stomach cramps.
The doctors fought the illness with their skill,
But it was stronger than the healing arts.
And so the fate that comes to all men came   870
To many; lords as well as clients died.
Oh sorrow! Frederick's losses were so great.

Since animals were hit by the disease,
The groans of mighty horses in their stable
Increased the pain of men who watched them die. 875
King Frederick was amazed by the destruction,
And to God who rules the heavens and the earth
He offered prayers up in a shaky voice.
"Almighty God who rules through all the ages.
O highest One, who governs all creation, 880
It pleases you to give me earthly power,
Unworthy as I am, to rule the world.
O holy One, bring help for our affliction,
And, Father, place a limit on our pain.
To save or to destroy is in your power, 885
For life and death are in your hands alone.
Grant us, your slaves, the gifts of your salvation.
May your right hand restrain the frightful slaughter
To let us see our fathers' homes in peace
And make an offering for our safe return." 890
So God the Father in his mercy heard him
And looked with kindness on his tear-stained face.
The savage plague then ended, and health returned
Into their weakened bodies by God's grace.
He left the place of pestilence and went 895
To visit other cities in the region,
Where he sought the tribute owed the Roman
   king.
The loyal people welcomed him with honor
And gave him gifts beyond what he had asked.
One city, it is said, had spurned the king. 900
Spoleto, a place that teemed with men and wealth
Is said to have committed fraud by paying

What she owed in counterfeited coins.
They also robbed a Tuscan count named Guido
While he followed in the footsteps of the king,　　905
And these two things were said to be the cause
Of Spoleto's ruin. The king was much disturbed
By these events, and he commanded them
To send the leaders of their town to him.
He wished to know the reasons for their actions　910
And whether without fraud they would obey
Their lord, who was prepared to forgive them.
These culprits feared because of what they'd done
(A guilty conscience always brings distress),
And they refused to budge and go to him.　　915
These stupid people scorned his right to govern.
Thus seeing himself spurned, the monarch rushed
There, for he thought the citizens would come
And meet with him to ask for peace and pardon.
Then peace and pardon he would surely give
　　them.　　920
But the proud and reckless people of Spoleto
Prepared for battle. Trained in shining arms,
They left their walls (impelled by evil fate)
And thought they could repel unconquered
　　Frederick.
The monarch saw they were prepared to fight him,　925
And said indignantly: "Behold, my knights,
They take the field, and we must use our strength.
You see, this haughty race prepares with arms
To keep us at a distance from their city.
Like fools, they do not fear to scorn the law.　　930

O mighty warriors, rouse your courage. Break them
And they'll regret they ever wanted war.
Make an example of them so that others
Will not dare to cheat the Roman king."
The soldiers were inflamed and rushed to battle,   935
As a lioness who was deprived of cubs
Will rage against the swords and scorn her wounds.
They killed the first who put up a defense,
But others fled and headed for the walls.
The Germans pressed those falling back and
   mixed   940
With those who entered through the open gates.
They robbed the city and its haughty people
And filled the town with sorrow and confusion.
Then mothers cried and babes and unwed girls.
The old complained that fate was savage to them,   945
Because by living they endured such pain.
The city with its opulence was ruined.
Spoleto was despoiled of all its riches.
So nothing more remained, because the troops
Had taken all and left the captives bare.   950
Their liberty alone the king had granted
To those who dared defy their royal master,
And the troops enriched with plunder went away.
Fatigue and death pursued these wretched people,
Whose sole possession, life, was lost by many,   955
And the teeming city now became deserted.

MEANWHILE the savage people of Liguria
Began their lawless battles as before.
Milan attacked her neighbors more than usual

And harassed those wretches who had made
   complaints.   960
Dishonest Brescia moved on Bergamo
And captured some of their unwary people,
Confining those who wished to keep the peace.
The Bergamasks in council then decided
To send the king their legates on this matter,   965
Who'd make complaints and put their case
   before him.
The legates quickly hurried to the camp
And made their plea before the royal court.
The pious Frederick listened to their problems
And sought the reasons for the Brescians' malice,   970
Since it appeared absurd to start a war
And suffer so much pain without a cause.
The legates gave this answer to his questions:
"What we say, O gentle ruler, is the truth,
For there is nothing hidden in our speech.   975
There used to be twin heroes in our district,
Who both had serfs and riches in abundance.
They were related and of equal rank,
And Mozzi and Brusati were their names.
Their families flourished by their honesty.   980
But when a quarrel flared up, one of them
Asked quickly for our aid. The other went
To Brescia and requested its support.
So Brescia gave its help to Brusati,
While Bergamo assisted his relation;   985
And thus they fought a long and cursed war
In which each people chose a different side.
Both cities suffered much, and the destruction

From this struggle cost the lives of many men.
This was the start; from here the hatred grew,   990
And a tinderbox of anger was created.
Tired and broken by the war, the leaders
Decided to agree on terms for peace.
Desiring to avoid a future battle,
Brusati tried to sell some splendid castles,   995
Because those places had been soaked with blood.
He told the Brescians many times that they
Could buy them, if they wished. If not, he'd cede
Them to the Bergamasks or sell them outright.
Since Brescia had refused to make the purchase,   1000
Some of our people took them for a price.
This news had bitterly enraged the Brescians,
Who soon began to move towards war, and fiercely
Did they threaten to harass, unless they gave
The castles back, the citizens who held them,   1005
As well as all the other Bergamasks.
Since Bergamo had wanted peace not war,
We said that we would take our case to court.
But never would we yield without a judgment.
This discord, pious king, has lasted long.   1010
Both sides have often borne the weight of evil
Fortune, and both are mourning many dead
Whom dread Mars gathered from this shifting
    struggle.
Yet soldiers who'd been captured in a battle
Were soon permitted to return in peace,   1015
And both sides would obey the rules of war.
Now Brescia falls upon unwary men
From Bergamo, who follow your commands,

And some of those remain within their jails.
And our manors are still open to attack.   1020
Therefore, our father and most gentle lord,
We bring our case before you for your judgment."
When they had finished, Frederick wrote an order
Commanding Brescia to release her captives
And end the war that she had undertaken.   1025
But if they wished to make a legal protest,
They should come in peace and not forsake
    their rights.
The legates from the Bergamasks returned
In joy, because they had fulfilled their mandate.

KING FREDERICK wished to see his home
    again,   1030
And on the way Ancona welcomed him.
He spent a few days there with his commanders.
The lord of rich Byzantium had sent
Most generous gifts of gold and silver talents,
Horses, copes, and garments to the king.   1035
He promised that he would send more if Frederick
Would agree to make a bond of peace with him.
He wished the daughter of his son might wed
The king, so that by marriage he might share
In Frederick's love. But fate did not permit it   1040
And prevented those twin rulers of the world
From joining forces by a wedding treaty.

SO HE FORSOOK this pact with Greece and went
Directly to Verona. To return
In peace, he took the route by which he came,   1045
Through the spot the peasants call Bolzano Pass.

But a band of evil men stood in his way.
The lofty Alps had long been captured by them,
Where a narrow path was blocked by their
    defenses,
And here a mountain, there a rushing stream.   1050
When Frederick and his host came to this place
And wanted to pass through, they saw the trail
Beset by rogues who were prepared to rob them.
The king addressed these foolish men as friends
And said they must forget their wicked scheme   1055
Of trying to prevent his men from crossing.
If they repent, he would forgive the injury.
Perverse these men who blinded by their greed
Disdained the king's advice to let him pass.
They wanted rich rewards for their compliance.   1060
Unconquered Frederick pondered what to do;
His subtle mind was wrestling with the options.
Surveying all, he scrutinized each recess,
And then the king conceived a daring plan:
Some men with swords would rush them from
    the front,   1065
While others in the rear would climb the mountain
And take those craggy heights the evil band
Defended. Quickly some knights grabbed their
    arms
And charged the crowd that watched the narrow
    pass
In hope of taking plunder from the column.   1070
The other knights prepared to climb and fight
An enemy intent on war and rapine.

Good fortune soon allowed the royal host
To place its standards on the mountain heights.
Seeing troops above and beaten down below,   1075
The robbers fled to hide in forest caves.
Some who knew the place escaped, but some
    were captured.
King Frederick cut their noses off the captives
And dug out eyes, and others lost their hands.
Mindful of their evil, they would fear the king   1080
And give example to all those who saw them.
The monarch crossed the Alps and went in joy
To Trent, from where he could return in peace
To Germany and his ancestral cities.

AND NOW, in one year's time, the golden sun   1085
Had completed its journey through the stars,
And the king returned to get a hearty welcome.
The people all ran solemnly to greet him
With a chorus dressed liturgically in white.
The young, the old, the children rushed to meet
    him,   1090
And everywhere triumphal celebration
Escorted Frederick on his way back home.
Then mothers offered prayers for sons who now
Returned, and smiling babies hugged the necks
Of fathers or grandfathers gone for ages.   1095
A woman long deprived of her dear husband
Was kissed as she had wished for many days.
All gave their thanks and praised the Lord of
    Heaven.
They celebrated at a joyous banquet,

For the king had come in safety with his men.　　1100
They also cried for those who were not with them,
Those killed in war, whom fate had borne away.
The noble father tenderly consoled them
And gave large gifts to raise their sagging spirits.

SINCE FREDERICK had no heir, his men
　　advised him　　1105
To lead a consort to the marriage bed.
And with God's help beget a pretty baby.
The kind commander followed their advice
And took the daughter of the noble Rainald,
For Venus did not have this virgin's beauty;　　1110
Minerva did not have her brilliant mind,
And Juno did not have her wealth. There never
Was another except God's Mother Mary,
And Beatrice is so happy She excels her.
The joyful Frederick with a host of nobles　　1115
Took his bride to Würzburg for the marriage.

BRESCIA HAD by then received the letter
Sent by the king on Bergamo's behalf
That tried to bring their struggle to an end.
But scorning their kind lord's commands,
　　that scum　　1120
Would neither stop the war nor free the captives,
And soon their hostile actions were increased.
Since they knew from past defeats their foe was
　　strong,
The Brescians were afraid to fight alone,
And so they begged and bought from everywhere　　1125
Great masses of both cavalry and foot.

For many nations lent their help to them.
Relying not a little on their strength,
At Mura they crossed into Bergamo
And wanted to destroy Palosco castle.   1130
The Bergamasks grabbed up their arms and went
To meet the enemy unaided, since
Milan withdrew the help that they requested.
The once beloved Cremona makes excuses
And blames her leaders for refusing aid.   1135
She mourns too late that she abandoned friends.
Both armies met and were about to fight
In fields beneath Palosco's meager walls.
For nervous troops the fatal hour had come.
But Brescia built a camp and stayed inside.   1140
In spite of all her men she was afraid.
But Bergamo displayed her troops and banners
Threatening war and vexed those men encamped,
Who often fled before them in the past,
With flying arrows, spears, and dreadful shouts.   1145
Although harassed, the Brescians stayed inside
And avoided battle with God's help, I think,
Because deceitful fortune was against them.
The sun gave way before the frigid night,
Whose cloudless sky was filled with clear
   moonlight.   1150
The men from Brescia thought to flee, except
Their shame and all those allies held them back.
The Bergamasks stood firm and taunted them
With shouts, because they held those men beseiged.
O reckless men without a cautious leader.   1155
O silly men, defenseless in the field,

Who failed to prepare a modest rampart!
Since one but badly sleeps upon the ground,
The troops had no desire to spend the night,
And many, fearing icy midnight air,   1160
Sought nearby houses. They would return, they
    thought,
By morning with their tired limbs refreshed.
But cunning Brescia spied on them by night
And learned how few were huddled near their fires
Without a rampart in the open fields,   1165
And how many now had gone away from camp.
So as the dawn approached, the Brescians armed
For war and struck before their foes regrouped.
Their strength dispersed, the knights from
    Bergamo
Withdrew. They felt the press of evil fate.   1170
But in great part the infantry had rallied
And fought with their accustomed savagery.
One troop had formed a wedge and violently
Attacked the Brescian foot. They cut them down
With keen-edged swords and forced them to
    retreat.   1175
The cavalry, however, saw their friends
Fall back and rushed to help with bridles loosened.
They tried to raise their spirits with these words:
"Stand firm! Why do you give your backs to them?
Though losers many times, this day is ours.   1180
For fortune favors us and God directs
Our swords. Already most of them have fled."
With shouts like that delivered at a gallop,

The knights restrained the foot and turned the
   tide.
On every side the Bergamasks were trapped.   1185
And look! Here the knights and there the foot
   attack,
But Bergamo refuses to give ground.
Instead she makes a stand in open field
And frustrates the assault of foot and horse.
(A few brave men against so many thousands)   1190
The air was filled with flying arrows, rocks,
And spears, while swords made shields and
   gleaming helmets
Thud like hail when it beats upon a roof
Or grain against a polished threshing floor.
And foreign nations say in praise of us: 1195
If Brescia fought alone she would have lost.
Yet fate was cruel and forced them to surrender.
The infantry refused to run but lacked
The strength to fight against superior forces.
Regretting the desertion of their friends,   1200
The cavalry regrouped and sought the war.
But Brescia was content to beat the foot
And left the field in joy to seek her camp.
Five hundred had been captured and a number
Had been killed, before they let the Bergamasks   1205
Retreat. They feared that God might change
   his mind
And take the palm that smiling fortune gave them.
But for Palosco castle's brave defenders,
Who were protecting it from hostile arms
And often blunting enemy attacks,   1210

This outcome was a frightful thing to see,
Since now they had no hope of outside aid.
They realized they could not hold the fort.
A meager palisade encircled it,
On which there blew a storm of rocks and arrows,   1215
And everywhere the walls had largely crumbled.
In sorrow they surrendered on condition
And freely left those ill-defended towers.
Remembering past defeats and how that day
A new camp was destroyed, the victors smashed   1220
The castle and avenged their ancient shame.
They then returned to home with many captives.
By time the dawn had chased the stars from heaven
All Brescia's joyous people came together
As customary for a crucial meeting.   1225
When it was brought to order, Consul Gerard,
Whose tongue was quicker than his mind, stood up
To speak. He gave his allies proper thanks
For help that Brescia needed to prevail
But also praised his townsmen to the stars.   1230
He said that in avenging their disgrace
They showed themselves to be their fathers' sons,
And urged them to be generous to the Church.
He ordered it recorded in their annals;
So every year their joy might be recalled.   1235
He believed the prisoners should be held until
The fortress at Volpino was returned.
Moreover they must swear not to complain
Before the king and not to break the peace.
With claps and shouts the populace approved,   1240
Intoxicated by the happy outcome.

One citizen, a wise and noble man,
Who in the past gave very good advice,
Rose up and spoke to them. His name was Lanfred.
"Indeed, most noble people, I confess   1245
That God Almighty gave great joy to us,
For we have conquered men with skill in battle
With whom we have disputed for some time.
So we ought to weigh our actions with great care
If we desire to build a stable peace.   1250
Yes, fortune can reverse our happy state
And give to vanquished men the victor's crown.
Consider your decision and beware,
Since Bergamo can beat us as she beat
Us in the past. If it be now your pleasure,   1255
Create a peace that lasts. Take good advice
And offer what is honorable like friends.
Reject the consul's plea and free the captives,
For a solid peace can never be compelled."
He finished but his words were not found
    pleasing   1260
By unlearned men who could not see their fate.
They acted quickly on the plan of Gerard,
Because they thought that Lanfred had been bribed.
So the weaker of two options had prevailed,
Like Achitopel and Hushai in the Bible.   1265
From them the son of David sought advice
About the business of his father's flight.
The Bergamasks embarrassed by defeat
Had come to hold a passionate debate.
Some wished to fight and to reverse harsh
    fortune,   1270

Abandon piety and leave the captives.
Yet others thought it better to obtain
Their freedom and to give Volpino back.
But sons and brothers put their families first,
And many lost their usual taste for war,   1275
Deciding that the prisoners must be freed
On any terms that Brescia offered them.
They sent the Abbot Manfred in great haste
With power to obtain the captives' freedom,
And so he met with Brescia's leading men.   1280
"You both are tired of this lengthy struggle
That caused your cities to endure much pain.
For savage Mars has taken many lives,
And both of you are holding many prisoners.
Bergamo knows the numbers you have taken.   1285
We cannot bring the dead back from the grave.
But captives can be honorably returned,
And Bergamo would keep that ancient custom.
O Brescia, give to me a proper answer.
Although your luck has let you spread your
    wings,   1290
Behave with your accustomed moderation."
The men from Brescia answered that with this:
"Bergamo knows the shame that she has caused us
By using lawless force to hold our castles
And plundering our people who were weak   1295
And did not have ability to stop them.
A fort we had constructed was destroyed,
And often many citizens were killed.
Defeated in past wars, we fled before them.
But now the power of Heaven has decreed   1300

That we avenge our sorrow and our shame
By beating savage Bergamo in battle.
To get the captives back, first please return
Volpino, which you hold against the law.
The fort belongs to us. That much is certain.　　1305
The prisoners will be kept until we have it,
And we will capture others, if God wills.
No longer will we suffer this dishonor."
The abbot sadly answered: "If your words
Are fixed, and there is nothing that can sway you,　1310
First swear to me that you'll give back the captives,
And I will see the castle is returned."
Their leaders took the oath as he had wished,
And many of their men were made to swear
To bind themselves more tightly to their promise.　1315
The castle was returned, but Brescia failed
To keep her word. Instead she forced the prisoners
To swear that they would not complain to Frederick
Nor to anybody else who held the power,
But to keep the peace according to the treaty.　　1320

46

BOOK THREE

BUT WORDS have wings that conquer highest
   mountains,
And these had roused the interest of the court,
About the way that Brescia broke the law
By striking Bergamo against the king's
Command. Also the people of Milan   1325
Harassed their neighbors more than usual
And had repaired the walls of proud Tortona.
This moved the pious king to holy wrath,
Since he recalled their previous behavior,
And complaints were coming in from everywhere   1330
That caused the anger of the prince to grow.
Since John Gandino did not take the oath,
He hastened to the king with rapid steps
To tell how Brescia lawlessly constrained them.
Bergamo's famous father, Gerard, did   1335
Not hide their shameful loss, and his complaints
Enraged the king and dukes. Unless she kept
The law and made amends to Bergamo
They believed Brescia worthy of destruction.
Como had the usual complaints   1340
And so did Lodi. Sad Pavia cried
That brutal Mars molested her most gravely
And captive citizens were jailed in chains.
Each city sought the reverend prince's aid.
The saddened father kindly promised help   1345
To all of those who justly had complained.
He would not let those crimes remain unpunished.

But first he wished to find out if Milan
Would honestly submit to his commands,
And soon he ordered legates to that city,   1350
Who told them to desist from evil war
And release the captives that they had in jail.
She also must permit the restoration
Of Lodi's serfs as well as Como's houses.
If they refused, his anger would be felt.   1355
When the people of Milan had heard this speech,
They praised the royal law with splendid words
And said they wished to faithfully observe it,
If it didn't violate their ancient honor
That other kings respected in the past.   1360
They blamed their enemies for their transgressions,
Since they did not initiate the war,
But rather they responded to attacks.
They wanted peace, unless great provocation
Forced them to seek a just redress through arms.   1365
They gave expensive presents to his legates
And asked if they could win his love for them.
But when the legates left, Milan, warlike
And indignant at the threats, most bitterly
Assaulted the people who complained. Not
   content   1370
With tribute, angry soldiers sped through fields
To where Lodi and Como once had stood.
They plundered all those wretches living there
Who had no walls and lacked the men to fight.
Whatever had survived was now destroyed,   1375
Not a human life, not anything,
Was spared, since even lofty churches fell.

They also robbed the priests who served the Lord
And smashed the noble bishop's spacious home.
They were indifferent to both age and sex.   1380
This conquering race then had their victims swear
To bear their yoke and its accustomed burdens.
Next they crossed the river and attacked the lands
Near the Ticino, where Pavia trembled.
Villas and castles were destroyed, and serfs   1385
Were taken captive. Trophies carried off.
The bonds of punishment were not relaxed
But grew much worse in spite of royal edicts.
So Egypt's king refused to free the Hebrews,
Nor would he make a sacrifice to God,   1390
Although he was admonished more than once.
He forced a heavy yoke upon them, since
His hardened heart rejected God's commands.
But then the Lord of angels freed the Hebrews
And brought them help in answer to their prayers. 1395
He drowned the king who suffered through ten
    plagues.
So the Ligurians who endured so much
(Although they saw their past complaints had
    harmed them)
Continued to implore unconquered Frederick
And asked that he might help them from the
    ground.   1400
The orator, Obzibo, crossed the mountains
And argued for the people of Ticino.
The young but learned Alberich spoke for Lodi.
In telling of the great pain they had suffered
That reverend man, Ardicio, Como's bishop,   1405

Who cultivated virtue in his soul,
Beseeched the king for Como and himself.
With eyes brim full of tears he made this speech:
"Unconquered king, remember the complaints
That I have often brought against Milan   1410
About that wicked nation's cruel oppression.
They will not let us dwell within our homes,
And now I'm forced to make more serious charges
Concerning dangerous men who test your laws.
Not long ago they swore before your legates,   1415
But after that they galloped to the place
Where Como stood, which once they had
   destroyed.
If anything had still remained undamaged,
It was completely wrecked or carried off.
For fire and sword let nothing go untouched,   1420
Including churches that had stood for years.
The clergy and the people both were robbed
Of everything except their lives. My house
Destroyed, I fled, surrounded by their curses.
But you who through the King your kingdoms
   hold,   1425
For the imperial glory, I beseech you,
Have pity and deliver us from pain.
May your right hand provide support for us."
So spoke the bishop. Lodi's legate then
Recounted all the woes that she had suffered   1430
And humbly begged the king to give them aid.
The eloquent Obzibo pressed those points
And goaded him to wrath with bitter words:
"Those evils that Milan's impious people

Inflicted on the cities of Liguria   1435
Are known to everyone, O pious ruler.
Therefore I shall not speak about those cities
Overturned or the people she compelled
To serve her. Have you heard about the neighbors
Whom she killed or how she robbed and has
    harassed   1440
The Bergamasks, Novarians, and Pavia?
Cremona too was crushed by hostile arms.
She saves her love for battle not for peace.
If castles were disloyal to their cities,   1445
She was prepared to offer them her help.
For Como's isle rebelled in just that way,
And Galeate wounded her Novara,
While Lisna dared to vex strong Bergamo.
Her armed support let Crema hate Cremona,   1450
And let her deny to Bergamo her due.
Why do these people violate the honor
Of the imperial name and scorn your law?
You saw their hatred on Tortona's ramparts,
Which then came crashing down with their
    defeat.   1455
Still in a little time they helped repair them.
But cities you gave orders to rebuild
Are refused permission and oppressed more fiercely.
Those felons harshly punish captives whom
Your piety commands to be released.   1460
They persecute those loyal to your laws
And demand the rights that rightfully are yours.
They are prepared to rule all of Liguria.
So offer us your help, imperial father,

And let your mercy comfort those in pain   1465
By ending the destruction of our towns."
This speech caused tears to flow down Frederick's
   cheek.
He gave his handsome head a shake and spoke:
"I see Milan must be restrained by force
To keep the peace and to preserve our laws,   1470
Which often love of power made her spurn.
It hurts me to have heard all those complaints
And yet not give to poor men some relief
Unless they give up war and show contrition,
We'll make those evil people pay their debt.   1475
They'll learn too late the power of the king.
You all should make a pact to band together
And pledge to give each other your support.
Now sweep away the terror from your heart.
For shortly we will bring the promised aid   1480
If God who rules all things will make provision."
So gentle Frederick gave them hope and solace,
Advising them to arm themselves with courage.
He also gave a banner that Milan
Would recognize and hesitate to raise   1485
Her sword against. Liguria was elated:
She thought Milan would end her wars, because
That city would not dare to strike the pennant.
But once begun, their madness would not stop,
And they raged against that banner in contempt.   1490
They acted like a stream that had been blocked
By one who wished to change the way it flowed.
But the water foams and rises uncontrolled
To break the high restraints that held it locked.

BOOK THREE

THEN FATHER FREDERICK thought to bring
    an army   1495
That would be strong enough to tame Liguria
And liberate his people from their chains.
Zealous was our lord to curb their pride
So that the peace and law could be maintained.
He called together all the dukes and magnates,   1500
And the leaders of Liguria also came,
Because their reverend lord was seeking counsel.
A multitude soon gathered at his dwelling,
And held a court. Then, sublime on his high
    throne,
The godlike king began to speak to them.   1505
"Right now we meet to face a serious problem.
I hope, my lords, you learn about its nature
And quickly give to me your true opinion.
The world once lived in fear of Roman power:
In places where the sun would rise and set   1510
No people spurned the emperor's commands
Unless they wished to forfeit all respect.
But now some in Liguria test our might,
And in their pride they violate our honor.
Milan's impious people crush two cities,   1515
Which once they had destroyed, and they refuse
To grant them their permission to rebuild,
Although their victims' cries moved me to ask them.
Pavia and her neighbors are harassed
By those who have no fear to scorn my laws.   1520
They did not keep their promise to my legates,
And my trip to Rome was marred by their contempt.
Now Brescia scorns my letter and attacks.

She forces careless Bergamasks she captures
To swear that they would not complain to me   1525
Or to anyone who can enforce the law.
Both people tread upon the royal honor;
They must repent or be destroyed, because
Our royal majesty has been insulted.
Consider this, my lords, without distraction,   1530
And help me to protect our kingdom's glory."
When Frederick finished, murmurs filled the air.
The leaders were divided. Many were
Offended and thought the king had borne too much
Without his taking vengeance on her pride.   1535
There were a few who wanted to excuse her
And moderate our furious leader's rage.

....
....
....   1540

To hasten to protect his royal glory,
Claimed by the evil people of Milan.
They promised on their honor their submission
To the king, if he would come with troops
And punish those proud men with brutal war.   1545
So they were all agreed to send a column,
For it was right to bring Milan to heel.
That city, which had scorned the royal edicts,
Stood condemned of charges made against it.
Then they annulled the treaty that the Brescians   1550
Had forced the captive Bergamasks to swear.
They were declared to be false citizens
And foes of Rome, who spurned their generous
   king.

They would not keep the peace and broke the law.
Then by an ancient custom Frederick raised 1555
His standards, and he praised his magnates'
 counsel.
Then quickly, at the king's command, the nobles
Swore to join their battle strength to his.
They chose the day when each must be prepared
To travel with their lord to Italy. 1560
Ligurians subject to the noble Frederick
Vowed to prepare their arms most zealously.
So they would bring their prompt support to him
And take, of course, what captives that they could.
Against accursed Milan they should give battle 1565
And bring Pavia all the help they can.
Bergamo and Cremona then received,
As they had asked, a royal mandate that
Gave to them the right to issue coins.
Encouraging knights, he ordered arms be readied 1570
And whatever else the war might soon require.
Now the assembly ended, and each returned
To gather what was needed for the battle.
The news of this campaign then spread throughout
The realm. It promised wealth and rich rewards 1575
For those who traveled with the king. The royal
 legate
Never ceased to rouse his magnates and to bear
His mandates through the towns. So men who were
Inspired by unbounded hope and praise
Declared to Frederick their desire to follow, 1580
And to those anxious men the wait seemed endless.
Arms, banners, clothes and horses were prepared.

Their bows were bent, and dirt was wiped from
   spears
And lethal swords. They fitted iron on
Their chests and clanging greaves upon their shins 1585
And fastened shining helmets to their heads.
They covered shields with hides from slaughtered
   bulls,
And minds were cleared of everything but war.

AMONG THOSE SUMMONED was a Polish duke
Who had prepared no arms to serve the king.   1590
This hard man had contempt for royal mandates
As well as for his family obligations.
He chased his brother's children from their land,
Although he knew they were the king's relations,
So he could hold it by himself alone.   1595
This wicked deed had made Augustus angry,
And Frederick went to Poland with his knights.
Since words and prayers could not convince
   the duke,
The king prepared to force him to obey
By ruining towns and fields and robbing
   peasants.   1600
The duke was driven to a lofty castle,
Impregnable to Romans in the past.
For nature and the hands of men had made
The fortress seem impervious to force,
Provided it was properly defended.   1605
King Frederick followed and besieged the castle
Until its desperate leader had surrendered.
He sought forgiveness and received that which
He sought by the entreaties of the nobles.

He swore fidelity and said he'd come   1610
On the campaign that troubled all of Gaul.
King Frederick, Rome's imperial glory, then
Demanded his obedience for life.
Once peace was made, the victor left in triumph.

MEANWHILE, Milan's hard people had attacked   1615
Pavia, for they did not fear to scorn
The banner that was given to protect her.
Nor did Milan believe (as rumor had it)
That Frederick would return to curb their pride.
She did not think there was a man who could   1620
Coerce this mighty nation to obey.
Therefore they raged in blind and senseless fury,
Like women rushing to a bacchanal
Without concern for husbands or for children.
A famous castle, lovely Vigevano,   1625
Had strong defenses and was filled with treasure,
Which the Ticinese were closely guarding.
Of all the forts that stood near the Ticino
It alone had lasted through attacks
That fierce Milan had made against this area.   1630
Obsessed with thoughts of war, that city launched
Assaults that several times they had repelled.
But now she gathered all her many allies
So that she'd have strength to take the fort
Without a thought that she would be defeated.   1635
Brescia was invited and gave help
To friends who asked with heartfelt prayers and gifts.
They did not fear our leader's blazing standards.
Obnoxious Crema sent what was expected,
For with Milan's support she scorned Cremona.   1640

And Piacenza and remotest cities
Gave their help. Thus countless troops had rallied to
The banner of Milan, who yearned to take
The castle that Pavia was determined
To defend. Then all prepared to cross the swift   1645
Ticino on a new bridge that Milan
Had carefully constructed for this war.
This caused the youth and Ticinese to arm
And rush to the defense of Vigevano
With the banner that King Frederick gave
    to them.   1650
They made camp in the middle of the field,
And boldly thought they could repel their foes.
For the Count of Montferrat had favored them.
They hoped Cremona, who had promised aid,
Would be their ally in the coming war.   1655
But Piacenza would not let her pass
The border. Blinded by the love for gold,
She wanted heavy tribute for the privilege.
Milan had offered bribes (so rumor had it)
In order to prevent the troops from crossing.   1660
O cursed greed, the pestilence of souls.
O lethal vice, attractive to the crowd.
O avarice that grasps the human race
Like a disease and holds with an obsession.
Therefore Cremona could not offer help,   1665
But still she crossed the border of Milan
To burn and devastate some of her castles.
And now two armies stood prepared to fight
With no great space between opposing camps.

Their shining banners caused both sides to
    marvel, 1670
And arrows filled the air as columns met.
The clamor reached to heaven and the camps
Roared in confusion. Savage hearts were pounding.
First prompting one and then the other army,
Fortune guided swords and goaded laggards. 1675
But Milan in fear withdrew her foot and so
Delayed her fate. They were advised to wait
And hold them back. This raised Pavia's spirits
Who was now massed and flying Frederick's
    banner.
Yet all were soon enflamed by all that shouting. 1680
With burning hearts they rushed to seek the battle.
The noble nation of Ticino ran
To meet the hostile arms that were approaching.
A monstrous war began. They fought with swords
And missiles, spears and clubs and flying arrows. 1685
Their shields and hollow helmets rang, while
    streams
Of blood and perspiration soaked the ground.
The earth was strewn with bodies here and there,
And horses fell from blows aimed at their legs.
I will not try to tell of each misfortune 1690
Or speak of every tear or funeral mound,
For I must hurry on to other things.
At first inconstant fortune helped Pavia;
The fickle goddess pressed the other side.
Young Ticinese had gathered troops and forced 1695
Their foes to run before their rising strength
For overwhelming power stopped Milan.

But soon the pick of her young men brought help,
And fortune turned to lend a hand to them.
Like heavy snows the throwing spears were flying   1700
Everywhere, and bitter war surged back again
In all its violence. The Ticinese,
Abandoned by both God and fortune, fall
Before Milan, and fearing open country,
They hurry to a camp that is too small.   1705
Surrounding them, the victors laid a siege
And were prepared to take the fort by storm.
Vintelmo soon arrived. He was a man
With skill at making instruments by which
A fortress might be captured or defended.   1710
He boasted that unless there was a threat
Of open battle, neither castles on
A plain nor cities could resist his genius.
Although his skills were bought for no small price,
Milan received and cherished him as if   1715
Vintelmo were their leader and their lord.
Indeed his art brought many triumphs to them,
Since well-protected castles often fell.
When he began to make his preparations
To seize the fort, its young defenders laughed,   1720
And girded the enclosure with sharp stakes.
They thought they'd men enough to hold
   the ramparts.
Yet their numbers made defense more difficult,
For hunger gnawed at those confined so closely,
Who laid aside their ancient love of war.   1725
If supplies sufficient to their needs had been
Prepared, perhaps the castle still would stand

With its imposing ramparts still intact.
Instead a savage hunger forced those men
To ask for peace and trust their enemies.   1730
How sad! All thought it best to kneel and pledge
Submission to the talented Vintelmo.
With hostages they ratified the peace.
Without delay this unjust judge then ordered
Machines be made to overturn the castle.   1735
He gave back to the Milanese the captives
Whom brave Ticino's soldiers took as prisoners.
The castles that those people held in malice
Would now be given over to Tortona.
He added penalties and kept some back,   1740
Which he said would be applied in better times.
He ordered that the sureties be kept
And those last captured locked in ankle chains.
Thus sadly did the Ticinese depart
In peace, a peace of words devoid of substance.   1745
For the precepts of this unjust judge oppressed
    them,
And they were not agreed to keep their word,
Although the captives' pain moved them to pity.
So their opinion still remained divided.
Some thought it best to keep their pledge
    of peace   1750
And have the captives freed from their
    confinement.
But the honor of the city and the crimes
Not yet forgotten caused others to desire,
With Frederick's promised help, to smash this
    peace.

One is amazed to learn the captives urged   1755
Them to reject a treaty that would mar
The glory of Pavia's reputation.
Indeed disgrace was worse than death to them.
Though late, they spurned those harsh commands,
Abandoning their prisoners and their bail,   1760
And broke the peace that they had sworn to keep.
Without delay the wise Obzibo rushed
To tell the monarch all that had transpired.
He humbly asked that Frederick quickly bring
The help that he had often promised them.   1765
Unless he brought them aid, their citizens
In jail could all be slaughtered, and Pavia
And the other nearby towns could be destroyed.
The legate and the royal chancellor, Rainald,
Whose probity had earned him his position,   1770
And worthy Otto, Count Palatinate,
Were sent to Italy by father Frederick
To win the hardened hearts of the Ligurians.
They reported proud Milan and certain others,
Including enemies of Bergamo,   1775
Refused to give obedience to him.
So the king should come to tame those shameless
    people
And speed his help to his defenseless friends,
For he must protect the honor of Liguria.
On hearing this the pious father ordered   1780
That from all regions arms and captains gather
Who long had ached for an Italian war.
Soon troops and men with power came together
From everywhere to form a mighty army.

Franconia offered Frederick many counts,   1785
And Suevia sent a force that was not small.
Bavaria was despoiled of all her bravest,
And Saxony would give her strongest men.
Bohemia gathered knights with glistening arms,
And Frederick ordered that her lord be crowned   1790
To gain the honor that his merit earned.
The number of the dukes could not be counted,
Nor could one speak of all the peoples there.
Now teeming Germany became a desert.
From everywhere fierce youths and nobles
    gathered   1795
To follow after Frederick's shining banners.
Now Phoebus reached the limits of crouched
    Taurus
And saw that Gemini was rushing near.
The farmer now rejoiced to see his harvest,
And he prepared to give his thanks to God.   1800
Leaving his wife behind, the Roman king
Began his journey with a host of knights.
Some frightening news was spreading
    through Liguria,
And a hundred tongues were bearing dread reports
That mixed the truth and falsity together.   1805
They said the column that King Frederick led
Was filled with countless dukes and bands
    of knights;
No king before had led so many thousands.
His savage men would bite their foes like beasts
And mangle human bodies with their teeth.   1810
They fed on blood and uncooked flesh. Their bodies

Were a frightful image, horrible to see.
They had no fear of battle or of death,
And piety or conscience could not move them.
They said the king intended them to rape   1815
The cities that he hated in Liguria
And every other town in Italy.
Liguria quaked with terror at these rumors,
And quickly girded ramparts round their cities.
Old walls received the care that they required;   1820
Deep were the moats that they would dig
   around them.
Although emboldened by their recent triumphs,
The Milanese still trembled when they learned
Of his approach because of all those stories.
Not knowing what to do, they asked Vintelmo   1825
To show them how they might protect themselves.
On his advice, they strengthened their six gates
And dug a good-sized trench. Above this moat
They built a palisade with greatest effort.
This huge work was immense, for it included   1830
The ancient walls and vast suburban tracts.
As the horror of these frightful rumors grew,
About the barbarous troops who were approaching,
The citizens the city paid to hold
The castles and the bridges in the area   1835
Were ordered by the people to return.
They had begun repairs upon Lomello,
Which hostile fate now forced them to abandon,
Regretting all that wasted time and money.
Tortona used her peasants for defense   1840
So allies might return back to their city.

64

But beautiful Maleo was destroyed,
Which Cremona had attacked before in vain.
They also ruined a bridge of planks and beams,
Whose cost and labor strained them to their
   limit,   1845
For Vintelmo built it large and with great skill.
The citizens returned back to their homes
And let the forts and bridges stand abandoned;
The frightened peasants fled the countryside,
And great Milan could scarcely capture them.   1850
Just so a hostile band of wolves will feast
By trapping and attacking herds of cattle.
But if by chance it sees some bears approach
From woods or hills, it leaves its den and runs.
And so the she-bear flees the raging lion.   1855
Strategic forts and citadels on cliffs
Were rarely manned and often left deserted.
For stories spread a dreadful king was coming,
Whom mighty cities barely could resist.

AND IN THIS WHILE King Frederick crossed
   the Alps   1860
And in your fields, Verona, made his camp.
He rushed there with a host of countless knights,
With which he dared to curb Liguria's pride.
As quietly he rested tired limbs,
The bright image of Milan appeared, and raised   1865
Her towered, trembling head against the night.
Around her seemed to mill a crowd of men,
Both young and old, whose dress showed great
   refinement.

65

She was a woman, old but beautiful,
Whose crown of towers gleamed with gold and
   jewels,   1870
And to our astonished lord she deeply sighed:
"At last you come, O Frederick, to besiege me.
They say you wish to fight and in your hate
You gather troops to violate my honor.
Who has persuaded you to take such actions?   1875
Who, I ask, is author of this evil?
He did not think who sent you as my foe;
More beautiful am I than other cities,
Liguria's best, the graceful seat of kings,
And rich in treasure, gold and silver metal,   1880
Rich in lineage, with land and power.
Don't spurn the words by which I try to turn you,
For countless knights and people honor me,
And the only fear they know is that which they
Inspire. The pope and king of Rome had loved   1885
Me once, since they preserved my ancient glory,
And both in turn received my loyal service.
Hard-hearted man, why do you spurn my gifts?
Why is your hate for me, my lord, so strong?
I want, of course, to follow your commands,   1890
If you would not refuse to give me honor.
Reject those false complaints, O reverend father,
That people from Liguria made against me.
For if you trace the sources of this trouble,
You'll find that we are innocent of blame.   1895
But if our prayers and gifts do not convince you,
If you persist in rigid opposition,
You'll learn my courage and strength in horrid battle,

For I have horses, swords and brave young men."
She spoke these words and vanished in thin air.   1900
The troubled king long pondered what he saw,
And lightly in a torpor was he held.
When it was over, Frederick rose and went
To softly pray and hear an oracle.
"Eternal God who justly rules the world   1905
And gives to each created thing its form.
Because You love the good and hate the evil,
Your majesty rejects those wicked men
Who do not wish to follow pious laws.
You cannot be beguiled by prayers and gifts,   1910
Since neither words nor cunning will
  confound you.
Rule me, I beg, teach me the way to beat
The treacherous foe who always trusts deceit.
You gave to me the Roman scepter, Father,
Although I was unworthy of a crown.   1915
Protect what you have granted, greatest King.
Allow me to defeat those savage people,
To rule in peace the humble and restrain
The proud. But if You are disgusted by
My sins, give me a sign of what will come."   1920
A voice from heaven thundered as he finished:
"Complete the course you started. Do not doubt.
Bring peace to pious men and war to sinners
And cleanse the kingdom, Frederick, of this evil.
Unless you fail the rule of law and justice,   1925
Unless you are seduced by bad advice,
I'll give to you the victory you seek,
And power will be yours for many years."

The pious king rejoiced at this prediction
And gathered his best knights to share his secret.   1930
He begged and urged them to preserve God's law
So that the victors might depart for home
In triumph with Liguria left in peace.
On their advice he sent his legates back
To ask the enemy to reconsider   1935
And to submit to laws that they had spurned.
For he could use his battle strength to force them,
Although he'd rather grant them his forgiveness.
As usual those felons gave their word,
But conscious of their guilt, they would not keep   1940
His just commands and would not bow before him.
And Frederick's mind could not be changed
   by gifts.
So did Jerusalem refuse a king,
For she would not submit to man's entreaties.
But her countless sins offended God, Who let   1945
His chosen people be besieged and captured.
He had given them great honor in the past.
While Frederick and his magnates were discussing
What each had thought and planned for the
   invasion,
Behold, the leaders of Cremona come   1950
To court and bear the mandates of their people.
"All praise and honor be in your possession.
O Frederick, let your glory shine forever.
Our loyal people ask for nothing else,
And we beg the Lord to grant what we desire.   1955
Learn, O noble leader, that Cremona
Has lavishly prepared the tools of war

And so has done you an important service.
We promise to supply at honest prices
Both food and drink sufficient for your column   1960
Till the sun has crossed the heavens seven times.
And hundreds of our battle-ready troops
Will follow royal banners, if you bid it.
Come quickly with your sword and check
   proud men,
So peace may be established in Liguria,   1965
And the honor of your kingdom may be saved.
Indeed we want to give Pavia help,
As your piety had once commanded us.
With arms in hand we marched through
   hostile lands
And leveled castles and their largest manors.   1970
But savage Crema stopped us when she could.
Throughout our land they robbed and stole and
   plundered.
They vilely broke the peace they swore to keep
And brought their help to arrogant Milan,
Who, they knew, had long ignored your edicts.   1975
Therefore our people ask, most just of kings,
That Crema pay the penalty she earned,
For that felon is the cause of many evils.
Now adverse omens marked that castle's founding,
And after she submitted to Milan   1980
All concord left the people of the region.
The cities of Liguria will not find
A lasting peace till Crema is destroyed.
That fort attracts a crowd of evil men
Who hold no law and have no native land.   1985

They give Milan the rights they owe Cremona.
For men who like to hurt are gathered there
As well as serfs and those expelled for crime.
There robbery, fraud, and murder find a home
With luxury, deceit, and other evils.   1990
Destroy that place so worthy of destruction.
Don't let so great a crime go unavenged.
For then Milan will fall just like a cripple,
And Cremona will rejoice to be your subject
When you bring back the peace of ages past."   1995
Our gentle leader gave them hearty thanks
For all the help they promised in this matter.
He said that he would give them large rewards
And give to Crema what she earned in grief,
Unless she break all contact with Milan   2000
And change her ways by keeping royal edicts.
For nothing can be better for his spirit
Than to break a haughty people to the law.
The angry king then quickly raised his standards
And sought you, Brescia, by a rapid march.   2005
But the monarch of Bohemia had already
Ruined your fields, for he had left before him.
Then Bergamo obtained her time for vengeance.
At the king's command, they wasted castles,
    homes,
And towers, and they pillaged to excess.   2010
The tumult and the screaming shook the earth,
And terror found its way to every door.
The peasants fled to town or sought the mountains
But castles on the highest peaks were sacked

And could not help those fleeing with their
   chattel.   2015
The savage knights attacked with fire and sword,
Capturing forts and castles, burning villas.
Engulfed in flames, the air is colored black,
And everywhere the smoke inhibits vision.
The anxious men enclosed within the city   2020
Pleaded with the king to quell his fury
And asked if they could make their peace
   with him.
The legates whom they sent to him approached
And begged on bended knees for Brescia's people.
They claimed that they would now obey the law   2025
And promised to send presents to his leaders.
The king felt them unworthy of his effort,
Since he would free those languishing in jail,
And then he wished to curb Milan by force,
The source, he thought, of evil in the region.   2030
The counsel of his knights and prayers appeased
   him;
So he destroyed their fields but not their city.
If we could have a way to see the future
And mortals might predict the things to come.
Then Bergamo would have the love of Brescia,   2035
Who would have let Volpino stand in peace.
They'd not have felt our leader's angry lash,
Whom later they would cause to bear much pain
When they would make a treaty with Milan.

BOOK FOUR

ONCE PEACE had eased the anger of the king,   2040
It pleased him to absolve the Brescian people.
Then at his nobles' urging Frederick marched
Upon Milan to crush that haughty nation
And free the captives from their ankle chains.
For he had heard their numberless complaints.   2045
So when he had approached the river Adda,
Whose rushing waters sought the morning sun
And clearly marked the city's ancient border,
He saw close by the other bank a column
Grim for war and gathered in the fields.   2050
This host of men was ordered by the consul
To keep the enemy beyond their shore
And stop a crossing if by chance they tried it.
On the heights above the river, Frederick noticed
Many horses, men, and wagons with supplies   2055
Prepared to travel to the fort called Trezzo.
It was a castle on the river's bend
Where nature forced the Adda's course to narrow,
And two sides were protected by the water,
Standing high upon a ledge worn by the flood.   2060
The front was level to the open plain,
And the other side was higher, like a cliff.
Upon this site the ramparts were constructed.
In former times old peasants named it Trezzo.
When rumors told them royal troops
   approached,   2065
Fear gathered all the people living near,

Who dwelled in various places here and there.
They fixed the walls and strengthened the
  defenses
And built three palisades around the ramparts,
In hope of saving both their goods and person   2070
And of resisting Frederick when he came.
Fed by this hope, the crowd prevented flight
But welcomed all those many who had fled.
Now when they saw the gleaming royal banners,
They gathered arms and goods to fight the king   2075
As he prepared to cross the river bank.
They wanted to defend their country's borders,
But they saved a bridge against the consul's orders.
For arrogance will conquer stupid minds.
Since snow had caused the water to grow deeper   2080
And cover shoals that might allow a crossing,
He thought no one would dare to step into
A river filled with eddies and deep sand.
So people from Vaprio and Cropello
Ran and boldly shouted threats at Frederick: 2085
"O red-haired ruler of the German fury,
Turn from this path. You have no right to cross
The Adda, which protects our sacred nation
And will not allow a foreign foe to enter.
Take your rapacious army far from here,   2090
But do not take a step across our borders.
You'll die yourself or have to shed our blood
If you attempt to violate our honor."
The rebels shouted things like that and worse,
And in a rage they gathered on the bank.   2095
They tried to stop the royal troops from crossing

By hurling stones and shooting arrows at them.
King Frederick was provoked into a fury,
And goading knights, he ordered arms prepared
To force their way across the swollen river   2100
And take their vengeance on those haughty
   people.
The greater part were quickly in the water
And needed all their skill to breast the waves.
But some were swept away. With foot the king
In gleaming armor took the bridge and struck   2105
Those who opposed him with a naked sword.
Just so a beast who sees that she is trapped
By a band of hunters, working to restrain her,
Will break their spears on her hard chest and use
Her strength to shred their limbs. So did our
   monarch   2110
Rage in anger at the hostile spears
Of savage foes, who grinned when they drew blood.
Although they saw our leader's frightful sword,
They boldly stood and fought before the bridge
Until they learned his knights had found
   a crossing.   2115
For they could hear them coming from the rear,
And when they saw them they were struck with fear.
They turned and tried too late to wreck the bridge,
But Frederick was not slow to set upon them
And held the bridge by forcing their retreat.   2120
Unlucky troops, once so consumed with pride,
Now dropped their spoils and fled like men
   demented,
While royal soldiers crossed the stream and followed.

The victors vented fury on the peasants;
Now they despoiled many of their arms   2125
And goods. They bound their prisoners' hands
   behind
Their backs and sold them for a price like cattle.
Some jumped into the river where they found
The death they wanted to escape. Others
In desperation sought the fort at Trezzo.   2130
The victors were enriched by what was left,
And with Vaprio ruined, they held both shores.
Meanwhile the heavens turned and night arose
As the sinking sun was hidden in the waves.
The wise king then commanded them to camp,   2135
And sleep became a friend to tired limbs
Until the dawn rose up to chase the shadows.
Since serious problems bore into his mind,
The monarch could not sleep because of worry.
The day was just beginning when his magnates   2140
Left their camp to follow after him.
At Trezzo they built camps throughout the fields.
Surrounding it, they'd make the greatest effort
And take by storm the men within its walls.
Then wild rumors filled Milan with fear,   2145
And what they heard was spreading here and there
That German leaders and their reverend king
Were standing on the near side of the river.
And first they captured some of the defenders
Who wanted to protect their country's borders,   2150
And now the Germans were besieging Trezzo.
Milan's young men were anxious for a fight
And rushed for arms. Right then they would attack,

But reverend elders of the town forbade it.
A consul stopped the youth and shut the gate,　2155
Although he chose three hundred knights to check
The roads and find out what the king was planning.
These soldiers wanted to obey his orders
And drove their horses through the roads and fields.
The royal troops were closer than expected,　2160
And when they saw them, rushed to the attack.
They took those wandering carelessly ahead,
While others left their friends and fled in shame.
Returning to Milan from all directions,
They sadly spoke of all that was destroyed.　2165
The common people shook within their breasts,
And a sudden, boundless terror filled the city.
The rumors frightened those outside the walls,
Who fled to town, as did unwilling monks
Whom fear drove from their rural isolation.　2170
They lived as had the sons of Jonodad,
Whose father ordered out into the wilds.
They left the cups of Bacchus and their homes
And were not allowed to learn the skills of farming.
The infamous Vintelmo joined the king　2175
And left the city stunned. He either feared
Milan's destruction, or as rumor had it,
He had thought to cheat in a nefarious way.
Could he gain more by feigning to change sides?
Or perhaps the greedy man expected presents?　2180

MEANWHILE the king by war and siege
　　has struggled
To conquer those enclosed by Trezzo's walls.
But they opposed him with great resolution

And hoped Milan would give them her support.
And now one day has changed into another,   2185
And now the hope of future aid was gone.
For a legate from Milan had just returned
To say that they could give to them no help.
For they themselves were prisoners of their fear,
And everywhere they saw a horrid vision: 2190
An army that surrounded them with death.
So fearing brutal Mars would capture them,
The men at Trezzo watched as siege machines
Began to smash their homes and shake their towers.
Thus sadly they surrendered, begging pardon,   2195
And Frederick in his piety forgave them.
He let those men remove all their belongings,
And they could go whichever way they pleased.
He ordered soldiers stationed at the castle,
Which he preserved from ruin, and fixed
     a nearby   2200
Bridge, destroyed by those rebellious people.
Although rejoicing in his many trophies,
He gathered all his men and kindly urged them
To stay alert in case of any danger.
"Exult, my lads, and give the king his due,   2205
For we have done a deed to be remembered.
We beat them when they tried to hold the border,
And now the first engagement falls to us.
Behold the spoils! Behold the fruits of pride!
Behold the castle where that rebel band   2210
Of plotters was determined to resist me.
The ramparts of Milan lie down this road.
Prepare your swords and spirits for a battle."

With banners raised the king climbed on his horse
And boldly led his army toward Milan.   2215
So all the soldiers marched through open fields
With all their loot and horses in abundance
And wrecked what they could find with fire
    and sword.
The ruler of Bohemia led the van,
And Rainald held the rear with other leaders.   2220
In the middle was the monarch, where he kept
His eye on all and carefully arrayed them.
Just so a careful pilot on the sea
Will guide the rudder and adjust the sails.
First he tells his comrades what to do, but then   2225
He stops to think when signs become unclear.
At length and by an unexpected route
The royal column reached Milan. They camped
Beneath the palisades and planned a siege.
A group of knights with golden shields was told   2230
To stand on guard, protecting others who
Would build the camp and strengthen it with sod.
The citizens were murmuring in panic
And ran throughout the city to and fro.
For part of them desired to attack   2235
And follow fortune. But the others stopped them
And feared to venture out against the king.
A consul and the elders had advised them
Not to trust their arms and rush to battle,
But they should wait until the time was right.   2240
Although their shame and anger urged them
    forward,
They acted with one mind on this advice.

With swords in hand they crowded on the walls
And filled positions at the palisade.
They hurled rocks from slings and loosened
   arrows 2245
That carried death to those who were incautious.
They gathered at the gates to guard the entrance,
And some prepared machines for throwing stones
With which they frightened foes who stood
   nearby.
Boys and unwed girls had climbed the towers 2250
And pointed trembling fingers at his banners.
The matrons with their mournful voices sought
The temples to implore the help of God
And brought large gifts to saints to save their
   country.
The priests would veil the altars with their
   incense 2255
And try to placate God by sacred rites.
Yet fear and misery had filled the city.
Oh with what speed prosperity departed!
How quickly joy became entwined with sorrow!
Not long before the power of Milan 2260
Brought war and terror to Ligurian cities,
And everywhere she flexed her strength and
   triumphed.
But now without a wound her fear destroyed her,
And she endured the pain of changing fortune.
Once camp was made the royal leaders rested 2265
And then began to press by siege proud ramparts
Where formerly the bishop's meadow lay.
Right there I saw our leader's splendid tents,

Which barely stood beyond the range of missiles
And countless nobles scattered through the
    fields.   2270
The people who lived near Milan and others
Who resided in Liguria vied to send
Their help. They rightly favored Frederick's cause
And wanted to destroy that hated city
In order to avenge their ancient grudges.   2275
Now briefly speak, O Muse, of those who came.
There hastened youth from Lodi and from Como
Rejoicing now that vengeance seemed at hand,
And generous Pavia sent what troops
She could to win her citizens' release.   2280
Delighting in a show of strength and riches,
Cremona kept her word and moved to arms.
Illustrious Novara joined the fight;
So many times before Milan had vexed her.
The knights from Bergamo had rushed to follow   2285
Mighty Frederick, who had pledged to show them
    honor.
Unwilling Brescia also sent some men.
Verona, Parma, Piacenza came,
Together with Vercelli, Mantua,
And the famous knight of Montferrat.   2290
Indeed, Tortona with Milan's compliance
Had broken off their mutual alliance.
Respectfully she sought the royal camp
And lent unwilling strength to the attack.
She feared that angry Frederick would destroy   2295
The walls that took great labor to repair.
But Crema did not cease to help Milan:

She raged against and plundered Frederick's friends
And scorned his laws as much as she was able.
O fools, who did not see their doom rush toward
    them,   2300
Modena, Reggio, and the men who lived
In lands far from Liguria sent their troops.
Much of Italy had come and made its camp
To lay a siege on orders from the king.
There one could hear a hundred different
    tongues,   2305
And there men of a hundred different cultures
Submitted to their lord without a murmur.
Germans and the Latins took the posts assigned them,
And they threatened the besieged with death and
    slaughter.
They shouted: "Death to miserable Milan!"   2310
Behold, armed Milanese regain their courage,
And breaking quickly from the Roman gate,
They strike the camp Pavia chanced to settle
With Rainald, the adviser of the king.
Pavia's youth then boldly snatched up arms   2315
And prepared to push invaders from the ramparts.
No less did knights from nearby camps who heard
The shouting rush toward them and join the fight.
Despising foes that they had often beaten,
The Milanese dug in their spurs and charged.   2320
They struck them at a distance with long spears
Or fought them hand to hand with naked swords.
The royal army was not slow to trade
Them horrid wounds. The corpses of the horses
And many human bodies strew the fields.   2325

Both fought with all the strength of raging Mars.
Imperial glory and the royal power
As well as ancient grudges urged them on.
The other side was moved by love of country,
And the sweetness of the native soil helped.   2330
By now the royal ears could hear the battle;
So now King Frederick came in golden armor
With countless bands of valiant knights
    behind him.
He rushed to try his strong right arm in battle,
But night had drawn a dark and dewy curtain,   2335
And the enemy withdrew to seek their ramparts.
Then in pleasing words he praised his allies' efforts
And advised those weary men to rest in camp,
Where sleep could quietly restore their bodies.
But it was late when Frederick sought his tents.   2340
When dawning day began to cast its light,
He ordered dukes and bands of knights to arm
And gather in the middle of the field,
Aloft on horses, bearing shining crests.
Now his exultant knights pour forth and break   2345
From camp, just like the reverend king himself,
Who sought the field upon a mighty stallion.
Fine knights had come from everywhere
    but found
No war. The rectors stopped the Milanese   2350
From rushing out. Since fortune was against them,
They thought it was enough to hold the city.
The untrained masses manned the palisade,
While bold youths held the gates, and all obeyed
Their orders. Then our proud commander spoke   2355

Before his troops: "It's a disgrace that those
Who burned for war now hide behind their
   ramparts,
Since they were just demanding royal honors.
What happened to their energy and pride?
Now show your horse the field, if you are bold.   2360
Prepare to fight, if you can trust your arms!"
His friends affirmed his words by dreadful shouts,
And with crowds of knights he circled round
   the city,
Exploring hidden corners for an entrance.
Just as a bishop leads about the church   2365
A group of canons in a long procession.
First will come the banners of the cross,
And then the pious choir. So did the king
With his retainers ride around the city.
The Milanese, protected by high ramparts,   2370
Could see his ready troops and gleaming banners.
Safe behind the moat just filled with water,
They raised a frightful clamor and expressed
Themselves in ways that were both fit and foul.
They aimed the best part of their threats and
   curses   2375
At their Ligurian neighbors and the Latins,
Who cut them back with even meaner words.
But mothers with their children stood in fear
And followed with their eyes the cloud of dust
And the circling army. They prayed to God
   for help;   2380
For those who were not strong because of age

Or sex were frightened. The column gleamed
  with bronze.
Among its dukes beloved Frederick rode
With golden armor shining in the distance,
Like the rising morning star at rosy dawn.   2385
Close to the palisade there was an arch,
Built in marble to a marvelous design,
And it stood like a machine of war against
The Roman gate. It's said the ancient Romans
Put it there in order to preserve forever   2390
The glory of their conquest of Milan.
Fearing their fierce enemy might take it,
A consul ordered his best youths to climb
And fight from it as from a mountain fort.
Completing its procession round the ramparts,   2395
The royal army saw the lofty arch
And those who dared to hold it. They prepared
To storm the place with all their might, and tried
To frighten those proud men with shouts
  and arrows.
With eagerness the king approached the arch   2400
And at a distance shot a deadly arrow,
Which killed a soldier stationed at the top.
The clamor rose to heaven, as brave fighters
Rushed around. With shields locked they tried
  to break
The structure at its joints and shatter it.   2405
Some strained to empty quivers of their arrows,
While others were preparing catapults.
The warlike youth from up above showered them
With flying arrows, rocks, and spears. They cut

The ranks of armor and repelled the column,   2410
As if it were a fortress they defended.
The sun had now completed half its journey
And sought the ocean, when the kindly king
Advised his men to leave their heavy labors
And to restore their tired limbs by resting.   2415
Therefore the men went back to camp and rested.
Meanwhile the city youths had fled the arch,
Returning back into the town by night,
For they feared destruction with the coming light.
Yet some audacious men remained for days.   2420
And bravely held the arch although surrounded.
But Mars began to strike them with such force
That they surrendered to the king. Upon
The arch the victor placed a guard and brought
The savage battle to the gates themselves   2425
By pressing his proud foes with bloody slaughter.
Soon all the city hastened to the gates,
And armed men rushed to man the palisades
And to defend the ramparts with their swords.
Then strong young men who burned to fight
    broke out   2430
And traded wounds just like the rabid beasts.
They did not hesitate to give their youth
In order to defend their fathers' homes.
So bitter was that struggle near the gate
That he who cut was cut himself in turn.   2435
All sought the beauty battle gives to death.
The sky was clouded by the screaming rocks
And spears, and heaven quivered from the noise,
While flocks of arrows flew in all directions.

85

Dark gore was mixed with dust and perspiration,   2440
And life expired as the blood poured out.
Yet sharply did the royal host attack
Beneath the walls the Milanese, who were
Accustomed to besiege the gates of others.
At last black night restrained the warlike furies   2445
And forced those tired men to leave the battle.
The citizens recovered in their city,
And royal soldiers sought their tents once more.
Then noble father Frederick praised his allies.
Like a generous commander he advised them   2450
To get a good rest after all that action
And prepare their spirits for the fights to come.
He also had the ramparts ringed with fire
And his best guards watched bolted gates all night.
On his advice the others spread on carpets   2455
And enjoyed banquet and the gifts of Bacchus.
After, they refreshed their limbs with sleep,
While youths whose crested helmets gleamed
    with gold
Ran round in shifts to make the ramparts bright
With fire. They sang and danced the German
    way,   2460
As guards played games throughout the sleepless
    night.
The Milanese who held the palisade
Were watching from above and clutched
    their weapons.
Keeping guard on orders from their leaders,
They checked the gates and strengthened the
    defenses   2465
While shouting filthy insults in a stammer.

As bands of youths watched near the gates and
   ramparts,
The fathers and the senate made their plans.
The end of night that brought the dawning light
Moved soldiers to consume the day with battle.   2470
A month had been completed, and Milan
Was ravaged by this unaccustomed siege.
She saw disease and war take many lives
And longed to end their city's bitter pain.
While armed young men were manning gates and
   ramparts.   2475
A consul and the elders of the town
Considered in the middle of the night
How they might make a pact to end the war;
And many plans were offered in debate
Until a consul spoke his mind before them: 2480
"O citizens, I think you understand,"
He said, "the nature of our plight along
With me. How many evils we endure
From the anger of this savage German king.
We should forget the past and now consider   2485
What should be done at present, since this horrid
Foe destroys the fields we cultivate.
Undaunted, he cuts down the crops we nurture,
While homes and castles crumble into ash.
For all is overturned, and we have not   2490
The means, oh shame, or valor to prevent him.
Unfaithful fortune turns her head away,
And many allies cease to be our friends
As fierce Liguria plots to destroy us.
Imperial Frederick uses all his strength   2495

To press Milan and lay a siege against her
That no one thought him capable of doing.
Our people must endure disease and war,
And daily bitter fate is snatching many.
Now there is hardly room for graves, and dread   2500
And sorrow fill the city. God himself,
Who used to favor us before, seems angry,
And choirs of saints have left us and our temples.
So listen to the way we should be thinking.
Since we could not retain the ancient honor,   2505
And God himself opposes us, submit.
Let not our shame inhibit us from seeking
To make a peace and keep what we possess.
The Roman leader has the legal right,
If we but speak the truth, to govern us.   2510
Then why do we rebel against his laws
And God? We could send men to sue for peace.
Oh let's not flee the rule of this high king,
To whom the Lord Himself has given favor."
The fathers were unsure of this advice   2515
But at length they all approved of it.
And now the morning star brought back the day,
For golden dawn chased shadows from the night.
Soon legates with instructions to make peace,
Urged by the consul, hastened to the camp   2520
And sought the intervention of Bohemia,
Whose king was asked to mediate the treaty.
They tried to moderate the royal fury
And make a truce, once war had been renounced.
With honeyed words and pleas they had
   contrived,   2525

They pushed their mandates seeking peace upon
    them.
But careful Frederick, the imperial ruler,
Recalled their crimes and all their wicked deeds;
So he refused to hear the pleas of people
Whom he often asked in vain to keep the peace.   2530
But truly, prayers and counsel from his magnates
Swayed him to end the war upon condition.
He granted to Bohemia's king, in whom
His foes had trusted, the right to make the peace.
And the terms that he proposed to them were
    harsh,   2535
Since he was acting on the high king's orders.
He said that they should presently return
All captives, whom they kept so long in chains,
And pay the fisc five thousand silver marks,
Because they often dared to scorn the law.   2540
They must promise to be faithful to the king
And swear to keep his edicts from that day.
Without deceit, they should submit and not
Usurp the royal rights and break the laws.
They must also make a treaty with their
    neighbors   2545
To keep perpetual peace and give up war.
Three hundred hostages would seal the pact.
The legates, when they heard these things,
    returned
Back to the city. They told all they had learned
To those whom custom gathered in assembly.   2550
The terms of peace appeared more harsh than just,
But pain and adverse fate forced them to yield.

So bitter tears were shed for love of country,
And precious honor won by letting blood
Had to be abandoned by them now.   2555
Not otherwise do dearest children mourn;
With piercing sounds from deep within
    their breasts
They cry aloud in grief at mother's burial.
Milan then emptied prisons of their captives
And followed all the reverend monarch's
    precepts.   2560
Now there was peace whose terms were put in
    writing.

THE SETTING SUN had nearly run through Virgo
And hastened toward the balances of Libra,
When the ruler of Bohemia and his men
Went back to home. Since peace had been
    established,   2565
The people and the magnates asked to help
Were sent away with Frederick's hearty thanks.
Returning peasants, scattered through the fields,
Were busy with repairs of burned-out villas,
And happy serfs sought land they long deserted   2570
To sow with grain and plow with eagerness.
But wretched weariness and death pursued them,
As first it did those whom the king besieged.
Not only did cruel plague consume the farmers
Of Milan, but then through all the countryside   2575
And even in the city did it rage.
An unjust fate was taking many thousands.
But father Frederick, having saved his friends
And with Milan at last in yoke, commanded

The quick repair of cities she had ravaged.   2580
He went without his magnates and the host
To trace their ramparts and to lay foundations.
Those people, once oppressed, rejoiced and gave
Their generous leader worthy praise. They saw
Their prayers fulfilled, their hopes of many days.   2585
They yearned to work and eagerly rebuilt
The leveled houses and the fallen roofs.
Some cleared the entrances and littered streets;
Some fixed old walls and gates that numbered four.
No rest for men whose labor seemed so sweet.   2590
Thus Como rose upon her old location,
But Lodi on the king's advice was moved
To where the Adda flows by Monghezzone
And carried cargo ships on spangled waters.
There on the river bank at his command   2595
They built the august king a home and palace.
Not far away there was a grassy field;
Roncaglia it was called by the Ligurians,
And when the Roman king came to their cities,
He'd camp and hold a diet on that site   2600
To give his justice and resolve disputes.
Thus seeking counsel in accord with custom,
Prince Frederick traveled to that place and called
His mighty lords and magnates from Liguria,
As well as scholars from throughout his realm   2605
To solve by their advice some points of law.
This judge, this lover of the good, now cut
The legal knots and answered all complaints.
He even made new law to keep the peace
For all the nations subject to his rule,   2610

And they should always follow what is right:
Let no man take up arms or harm another.
Away with fraud, deceit, and crimes of theft.
So had men lived this way in the beginning.
Rejoicing they found heaven here below,   2615
And therefore it was called the age of gold.

INFORMERS often came from here and there
To tell of Piacenza's many crimes,
Which pushed our lord to anger. He commanded
That their walls be overturned, their moat be
    filled,   2620
And their ramparts be destroyed in expiation.
So grieving, they pulled down all their defenses.
Then Frederick ordered all Ligurian cities,
Once they had sworn an oath and posted bail,
To keep the law and hold his trust unbroken   2625
And not forget the duty owed to peace.
In safety he soon moved toward other towns
And left Liguria subject to his rule.
It now enjoyed a leisure without war.

PERVERSE ALLECTO mourned this spread of
    peace,   2630
Since anger, war, discord, and frightful crimes
Were the things she always found exciting.
She quickly left the lair of her dread sisters
And tried to break the bonds of hated peace
By stirring people to their usual frenzy.   2635
This hag adorned with serpents sought Milan,
And entering town, she tried the young men's
    hearts,

Inspiring madness that rejected peace;
Even children were infected with her poison.
She appeared in various forms as time
   demanded   2640
And shaped her speech to weaken wretched men:
"How will you ever win a reputation?
Is it for this a soldier's taught and trained?
Since leisure is effeminate and turns
Your courage to sloth, this idleness will take   2645
What strength remains. Made torpid by
   this peace,
You will accomplish nothing in your prime.
You, children born of men whose noble deeds
Have spread their reputation through the world
And made Milan most famous of all cities.   2650
Let their example animate your souls.
Let their achievements raise your sagging spirits,
For courage and glory bore them to the skies.
Degenerate is he who will not follow
The honor and the actions of his father!"   2655
With such a speech she goaded boys and youth;
Then to the elders, the lying fury turned:
"How great is now the shame," she said,
   "that men
For so long free and strong have bent like slaves
Before his yoke. Men to whom nations bowed,   2660
Whose brilliant triumphs showed the world their
   power,
Should not forget their liberty or honor.
O God! my reverend fathers, in your time
The glory bought by so much blood departs.

Your noble citizens will now obey,   2665
Oh shame, the orders of those haughty Germans.
By fate the lord becomes a household slave.
Brave men, can you endure to see this happen?
Better die than live a life dishonored,
For who with heart and manly courage can bear   2670
Proud masters and the arrogance of Germans?
They'll snatch up for themselves their subjects'
    goods.
They lack restraint and values and the sense
Of what is holy, and unless your fight,
They violently will steal all your possessions.   2675
They'll rape your wife and daughter in the street.
O Jesus. With your liberty forsaken
They'll crush you like a slave they bought
    for pennies."

ALLECTO SAW that with this speech all boiled
In her poison, and they were grasped by
    madness once   2680
Again. Then up on black wings she did rise
And rush to Piacenza like the wind.
Tranquillity, the friend of peace, was frightened
And fled as the impious fury entered.
She changed her savage face and twisted limbs   2685
And took a shape trustworthy and refined.
She spread her treacherous message in this
    manner:
"God brings to you the answer to your prayers.
Rejoice, my people, raise your listless spirits.
For, if you wish, you can remove this stain   2690

Of mockery and shame, this cause of sorrow,
Which lately has consumed the population,
When the wrath of that harsh tyrant smashed
   the walls.
Now put away unworthy fear, great people.
Build ramparts round this city so disgraced,   2695
For glory lost and liberty repressed
Can be recaptured with new walls and towers.
Once bound by love to you, Milan deserts
The treaty that the harsh king forced upon her.
She finds no honor in the service of   2700
Proud Germans who had savagely oppressed her.
Act now. The time is ripe. Do not delay!
Withdraw your necks from under his harsh yoke,
For such a life is shameful to free men.
Drive fear away, and grasp your former courage.   2705
Construct new walls, and gird the walls with
   ramparts.
For there is no one who can now prevent you.
The savage king who ordered their destruction
Is far from here and cannot summon allies
As before. Hurry now, for fortune helps you!"   2710
And so Hell's goddess with a lying face
Incited wretched men with reckless courage.
Soon the city was surrounded by new ramparts,
And deep moats, which had been filled, were dug
   again.
They raped the peace and rose against their lord,   2715
Refusing to obey a savage tyrant.
Indeed they rushed a legate to Milan,
Who made with her a treaty of alliance.

He sought her help and promised her their
    friendship.
NOW with her evil wish in part fulfilled   2720
Allecto rose into the sky like lightning
And went to Crema as the sun sank low.
She wandered through the castle in a rage
And frightened its defenders with this speech:
"Be vigilant! This is no time for rest.   2725
Don't trust this lying peace. A war begins.
The fierce king scorns the law and breaks the
    treaty.
Moved by Cremona's many gifts and prayers,
He plans to destroy you. I think I see
Across the field the walls of Frederick's camp.   2730
So now you must take courage up with your arms.
Defend your homes with your accustomed virtue.
Remember, I beseech you, how King Lothar
Had tried to take your ramparts in a battle,
But you repelled him with the aid of God.   2735
Again the help of Heaven will be given.
Have faith! Despise this harsh lord's threats and
    orders.
Be resolute in your defense of country.
This castle is coequal to great cities;
Don't let it fall without a shower of blood!"   2740
These words drove them to disobey the royal
Edicts. So trembling, they forsook the men
Whom Frederick held as bail and broke the peace
As rebels and the allies of Milan.
The lying goddess rose up in the sky   2745
And quickly flew, O Brescia, to your borders.

A legate of the people of Milan
Had come there to exhort those friendly people
To join their forces in a new alliance.
The fury laughed, since now her time had come.   2750
She changed her looks and strengthened
   wavering hearts
With words that moved them to a love for war.
"Great people, if your wish to keep your rights,
Your honor, and the freedom of your fathers.
Don't hesitate to join Milan as allies   2755
And break the treaty with that German tyrant.
For who could live a free man under him
Or bear the yoke of his unjust command?
Trust and be trusting. Take their help. Become
Their ally and repel this haughty lord.   2760
Great glory, praise, and honor comes to you,
Whom fate will place upon the royal chair.
Both nations will be safe if you unite,
And threats will never terrify you further.
For who indeed will dare to harm such allies?   2765
This news alone will cause all men to fear;
The king himself will tremble at its sound,
And he will be afraid to wage a war
Again. But if by chance he moves to arms,
He will retreat before your crushing strength."   2770
So Brescia joined Milan on her advice
And stupidly rebelled against the king.

BOOK FIVE

FROM EMILIA Frederick sent Milan his legates,
Since he was unaware the peace was broken.
They brought her friendly greetings and his
   orders   2775
And counseled her to keep the treaty's terms.
When rowdy youths saw the legates in the city,
Proclaiming orders from the hated tyrant,
They roared with indignation. In their fury
They scorned his law, and with their swords they
   ran   2780
To threaten them with death in shrieking voices.
The legates fled in terror to the king
And told him of the wrongs they had received
And what disgrace they bore, when rabid fury
Captured those he had subdued and made them
   rebels.   2785
Indeed they said that three Ligurian peoples
Allied themselves by treaty with Milan
Against the law of peace and royal honor.
When Frederick, the commander, understood this,
He proscribed the rebels and returned   2790
To war again. He ordered arms prepared
And summoned all the strength of his
   great kingdom.
The monarch sent a message to his consort
To gather bands of knights and leave the palace,
And come and take the blessed palm with him.   2795

They would enjoy the triumph after battle.
Soon the sacrilegious fury had returned
To trouble hearts among the Milanese
With words that she invented to incite them.
"Brave people, you intended to observe   2800
The royal pact, but wicked Frederick breaks
The treaty. In stinking caves he keeps in chains
The hostages you sought by the agreement.
He has proscribed you also, and now he calls
His vassals to prepare a siege against you   2805
That will lead to your oppression and destruction.
So listen if you wish to save yourselves.
At once your youth must grab their arms,
    and while
The savage leader lingers far away,
Drive out audacious foes within your borders.   2810
For Rudiger the Proud resides at Trezzo,
Who always harms whomever he is able.
We must beat him down in battle with
    our friends.
Now seek him; do not fear. This deed is worthy.
The fort is holding not a little treasure   2815
And rich you could become. So take up courage
And arms, for fortune is your ally now!"
Then from her hair she freed two snakes,
    whom she
Infected with the Gorgon's poison, and
She threw them at the doubters. The serpents
    slid,   2820
It's strange to say, through mouth and breast,
    but made

No contact, while inspiring them to fury.
Then she blared the trumpet that she carried,
Rousing all the city with horrendous sounds.
The young and old ran out with rustling
    weapons;   2825
The frantic people went through open gates
And rushed to Trezzo with their gleaming arms.
But the goddess of the underworld went first
To tell the castle that its foes approached,
Who'd capture them by force and raze the
    ramparts;   2830
And then she raised herself into the air.
Thus many with their faces white with terror
Rushed from everywhere to Rudiger,
Who in the end accepted their report.
He trembled but exhorted the defenders   2835
To stand before the ramparts with their arms.
He also asked the king to come in haste
And bring him help. A messenger was rushed
To summon nearby allies of the king,
Who quickly came to follow unjust fate.   2840
And now the frenzied people of Milan
Approached and laid a siege around the castle.
A frightful noise was raised into the skies.
The sounds of horns and trumpets mixed together,
While German youth manned ramparts and the
    towers   2845
And scorned those people's threats and empty fury.
A war began. Then arrows filled the air,
And rocks and missiles bearing death fell like
The snow or hail. The phalanx from Milan

Attacked with vigor, wanting to possess   2850
The fort before the king could help his allies.
The catapults were readied, and the boulders
That they hurled smashed the ramparts with
    such force,
And they whistled as they flew into the castle.
Some soldiers put their fear aside and climbed   2855
The wall on ladders that were joined together.
They wished to fight them hand to hand and had
One goal: to win. But those who fought
    against them
Were determined. They cut down with
    their swords
And pushed back those who tried to climb
    the walls.   2860
Upon the troops below, they threw whatever
They could find, like beams of wood or hunks
    of stone.
This rain of blows broke shields and shining
    helmets,
And on both sides the savage, roaring Mars
Was growling in a wrath that gave no rest.   2865
The warlike people of Milan continued
To attack both day and night, till Rudiger
Together with his allies had surrendered.
The fear of death had forced the German youth,
Oh shame, to leave the ramparts and to suffer   2870
The indignity of being bound in chains!
At once victorious soldiers ruined the castle,
And loaded with their plunder, they departed

With youths subdued by Mars held as their
  captives.
But father Frederick rushed with shining arms   2875
And hosts of knights to bring his allies help.
When he had learned the garrison was captured
And saw that Trezzo's walls had been destroyed,
He swelled with rage and almost lost control.
He would avenge dishonor as did David,   2880
Who saw the ruins of Ziklag through his tears.
He held it as a fief from King Achish,
When he left his native land in fear of Saul,
But fierce marauders took their wives and children
When David's men were off to fight a war.   2885
Without delay he wiped his tears and tracked
  them.
He found, he beat, he robbed that hostile band
And took back what it had perversely stolen.
Just so, with thoughts afflicted by his sorrow,
King Frederick chased the people of Milan   2890
And quickly ruined the fields they had restored,
Or that survived the previous destruction.
He devastated both the grapes and grain,
Just as a raging beast deprived of pups
Will rip whatever comes into her path.   2895
Then Frederick changed his course on the advice
Of nobles and the people of Cremona,
Who first would have him take the shameless
  Crema
So that Milan would fall with greater ease.
But then the virgin daughter of the night,   2900
Who wished to end her task and leave the light,

Flew directly to the Cremans' friends
And urged them to collect their strength and help.
She moved those men and aided them with arms.
Milan dispatched a cohort filled with allies   2905
For support, and Brescia also sent a squad,
Though many followed of their own free will.
Once fierce Allecto quickly drove them there,
Rejoicing in the evil, she departed
And hid herself in Hell, the dusky place   2910
From which she came. But on the king's command
The stalwarts of Cremona and Count Conrad
Exultantly besieged those hated ramparts.
The famous brother of the high commander
Placed his many soldiers near the western gate.   2915
Already war had sown the field with bodies.
Of course when Crema saw that hostile troops
Had come to lay a siege around their ramparts,
She ran audaciously with arms in hand
To resist by fighting in the open fields.   2920
Soon dead horses dot the ground; no help are they
To men besieged. The battle raged until
Those tired of the struggle sought their ramparts.
Before two gates the royal side made camp
And ravaged every kind of crop and vineyards.   2925
Now the high commander, Frederick, came
And fixed his tents against the eastern gate
Upon the sparkling river's sloping bank.
See, the sudden fury of a rising storm
Has snapped the ropes and knocked the tents to
    earth.   2930
The army of the winds has struck and wrecked

103

The royal camp, as if Aeolus sent
Relief to the besieged. But violence
Did not move the august king, who ordered roofs
Constructed to withstand the winds and storms.   2935
The nearby forests gave abundant wood.
And look! They built grand houses for their camp.
The wind also relaxed her savage fury.
The Bergamasks, so loyal to the king,
Rushed without delay to give their lord support.   2940
And all Liguria came to lend their strength,
Except the three Allecto had deceived.
So too did Beatrice bring the fiercest knights,
And a thousand vassals followed after her.
Distinguished by his birth and for his sword,   2945
Duke Henry led the noble Saxon nation
And placed his camp next to the northern gate.
The son of royal Conrad was close by.
He was a handsome well-built lad, who had
His father's virtues, although he was still young,   2950
But he was far away up in a fortress,
Where the sight of risky war would not
    disturb him.
Now Crema was surrounded by their legions,
And a machine for breaking walls was built.
The roar, the threats, the tumult of the battle,   2955
These horrid sounds were cutting through the air.
Yet the youth inside the fort, who held the gates
And manned the walls with arms, were hardly
    frightened,
Though their voices sometimes raged and
    sometimes threatened

104

The imperial troops in loud and vulgar language. 2960
No day was free from battle and attack;
Beneath the towering walls they traded blows,
And black blood flowed from the exchange
   of wounds.
So missiles, rocks, and arrows that were swift
Were falling like a heavy snow or hail. 2965
Each thought to fight or kill, not of himself.
On both sides raging Mars raised great confusion.
The love of home and country moved Milan,
While Frederick's strength and right to rule drove
   others,
And the hatreds of the past were not forgotten. 2970
They smoldered and they goaded them to action.
Often in the middle of the day, the youth
Broke out and yearned to fight in open country.
And often when the dark could offer rest,
They prepared to burn the camps around
   the fort. 2975
The fierce commander wished to terrify
The Cremans and confuse those hated people.
He ordered six young men to be suspended
By the neck and die upon the gallows.
When they had seen them hang, the restive
   youth 2980
Lamented, and at once they built a gallows
Where in a row they hanged four captive knights.
Thus they avenged their shame. Our leader glowed
With rage and quickly ordered hostages
Whom the rebels gave some time ago in hope 2985
Of peace be brought from everywhere to die

A wretched death before their parents' eyes.
There was a lofty tower made of beams.
Cremona had it built at great expense
So that it stood above the walls and ramparts;   2990
And rocks and arrows could be hurled below
If they could move that structure near the castle.
From this machine the king expected victory.
Against it, Crema made two catapults
Which struck, as fulling mills strike at the cloth,   2995
Both day and night with frequent blows.
Down fell the beams and nets, the boards
   and lattice,
And all the things that made the tower strong.
Then no one fearing death would stand upon it.
So Frederick was consumed with rage and took   3000
Unspeakable advice. He ordered those
Poor hostages be tied upon the tower
To suffer from the catapults' attack.
Once bound in place and facing death they cried:
"Beloved brothers, spare us please! Please
   spare us!   3005
Don't stain your hands on those you gave in trust.
But if you find no other way to save
Our walls, we will not flinch to give our lives!"
And with such words they uttered sighs
   and groans.
What should they do? Should they hold pity back   3010
And strike their friends, or let the dread machine
Approach the walls? Now if the tower reached them,
They feared both for themselves and for
   their country,

But they wept for those they saw exposed
   to death.
Since they hesitated in returning blows,   3015
The rectors urged them on with bitter words
To keep them busy launching rocks and missiles
And stop the enemy's approach. They thought
It best to fight and sacrifice a few
Than to permit the city to be lost.   3020
Encouraged by this advice, they shook their
   torpor.
In tears they struck the bodies of their comrades
And fought to drive the tower off with missiles.
They crushed their chests, their stomachs, and
   their heads,
And bone and mushy brain were mixed together.   3025
It was a savage, horrid thing to see.
At such a sight, the king, who now was calm,
Pitied those exposed to unjust fate.
He moved the tower back and freed the wretches.
Too late he scorned advice he took in anger.   3030
The besieged, who wished to bury the remains,
Asked his permission, and it was quickly granted.
They stopped the war and rested several days.
The king then planned to use the greatest force
To take his savage enemies by storm.   3035
First he had a tortoise built, and then he ordered
Men to fill the moat. So he could move that tower
Near the rampart and destroy those hostile walls.
The knights obeyed him and began to work.
Protected by the thickness of the tortoise,   3040
The commander took a spade as an example.

But from the walls above, the eager youth
Threw torches, missiles, rocks, and flying arrows.
They used what means they had to stop their foes,
But the tortoise could repel the rain of blows   3045
And let the knights continue with their labor.
The men who hurled in vain those rocks became
Exhausted, and the quivers that were emptied
Could not prevent the moat from being filled.
And now the column struck the wall and
    smashed it   3050
To make a passage big enough to enter.
Now frightened youth within, from every corner,
Ran to hold the entrance and to block the hole
With beams, and they prevented an intrusion.
The shouting from this battle shook the heavens.   3055
In all directions rocks flew from the hands
Of men, who also loosened arrows here and there.
At length dark night restrained their savage fury.
The vigilant Marchesius pretended
To be working on the wall while others slept,   3060
But then he left his place within the castle
And brought himself before the royal tents.
He either saw that Crema could not hold
And feared the retribution after battle,
Or thought that noble Frederick would
    reward him   3065
If he betrayed the castle's secret plans
And showed to him a way it could be conquered.
Renowned among the craftsmen, this man knew
All the plans and secrets in this fortress.
So when the light repulsed nocturnal darkness   3070

And it was clear Marchesius had left,
Wrath, fear, and sadness grabbed at the defenders.
Just as the sailors of a wave-tossed ship
That lost its pilot to the howling gale
Will quake with fear and tremble for their lives.   3075
The rectors tried to soothe the grieving crowd
And said the flight of one man did not matter,
Since men with skill and youth with courage
    remained,
Who could defend the castle with their virtue.
They urged them to return their thoughts
    to war   3080
And stirred them up with memories of their
    exploits.
These words inflamed the youth, and thus revived
By this advice, they formed a battle line.
They flew out and discovered that the tortoise
Was standing unprotected where the moat   3085
Was filled. So it was burned beneath the walls.
With spears and fearsome shouts they rushed to
    battle
And harassed their savage foes with all that noise.
The royal troops were quick to take up arms,
And hand to hand they forced them to retreat.   3090
They traded wound for wound, and blood
    flowed like
A brook in that cold massacre of men.
And when the whole camp rushed at once, the
    Creman
Crowd withdrew behind its palisade,
And there they fought courageously with showers   3095

Of stones, with javelins and feathered arrows.
Then the high commander ordered men to use
A great machine, so that his knights could throw
A bridge across the wall and burst upon them.
When soon they pushed the engine toward the
    ramparts,   3100
The Cremans could do nothing to prevent it.
But they could keep the bridge away and stop
Audacious troops from climbing on the wall.
Like hail the flying rocks were falling,
And every hand was ready for a blow,   3105
Since no fatigue or hardship held them back.
Anxious for a battle, Crema's youth
Ran to and fro and took their turn at fighting.
Now from the summit of the high machine
The soldiers threw their missiles in a cluster   3110
That fell like lightning coming down from heaven,
And rocks struck those who wandered through
   the castle.
The once too happy youth became confused,
And the fort was shocked to watch its ramparts
   fall.
The leaders, who were babbling in their terror,   3115
Could see how many met a wretched end,
And how many were so badly wounded that
They could not help, for death was drawing near.
The young men, who at first were bold and ready,
Now ceased to change the guard and feared
   the battle.   3120
They stopped their fierce attacks upon their foes
And spent a long time pondering what to do,

Before they called the populace together.
With mournful words they told them what they
   thought;
With flowing tears they urged them to surrender,   3125
Since a hostile God refused to let them stay there.
But the people loved the sweetness of their soil
And shut their minds to this advice. They said
That they preferred to die than to surrender
While men who still could hold a sword
   remained.   3130
The moon had finished seven revolutions
And had renewed its fire as many times.
Then the havoc of that engine so depressed
The Cremans, who by now desired rest,
That on advice they gave themselves to
   Frederick,   3135
If he would grant requests for peace and pardon.
These people thought Duke Henry to be honest
And requested that he mediate for them.
The noble king was moved by his petition
And gave permission for them to depart   3140
With what they still possessed of their belongings.
So Crema was deserted. Her wretched peasants
Took a few possessions as the king agreed.
Some traveled toward Milan, where they would
   lose
Again, but some had different inclinations.   3145
So then voracious fire, ignited by
The people of Cremona, burned the castle;
And temples, homes, and high walls crashed
   to earth.

Now Crema, once so mighty, lay in ruins.
Exultant was Cremona. Prayers were answered.   3150
Exultant were those loyal to the king.
The vassals celebrated and the name
Of sceptered Frederick was carried to the stars.

THE KING could think of nothing but
    the conquest
Of Milan and the remaining rebel towns.   3155
His mind was turned to war, and shortly after
He moved within Milan's most spacious borders
And devastated fields all around her,
Ravaging the vines and stripping trees of bark.
But the people were afraid to leave the city,   3160
And Milan endured the pillage of her land.
Then Frederick turned to Brescia, and like
    lightning
He struck what he found standing in his way.
There was a famous place, by name Iseo.
Rich with gifts of Bacchus and Minerva,   3165
It was protected by both man and nature.
Here stood the lake packed full with fish,
    and there
Tall mountains touched the sky. The narrow
    entrance
Was defended by a palisade and moat.
A hearty race had lived there once, who could   3170
Inspire fear but did not fear attack.
They stored in it a large amount of wealth.
A host of men in terror of the king
Had left their homes to gather in that castle,

Because they thought they would be safer there.   3175
A report had quickly come to royal ears
That all those splendid treasures in Iseo
Would soon be his, if he would come and take
    them.
So he urged his men to go with sugared words
And took the road to show the world his
    strength.   3180
But when they learned the savage king approached,
Those people quickly snatched up arms and ran
From the enclosure into the open field.
They thought, with any luck, they could return.
But now the monarch with his host was near,   3185
And angered by their warlike preparations,
He broke those people with his sword and spear.
His finest vassals raised a shout and followed;
One group of knights made for the mountain
    heights.
To come upon the rebels from the rear.   3190
These people, once relaxed and bold, were
    frightened,
And they regretted leaving the enclosure.
Yet still they rushed to war with shouts and fought,
But soon their terror forced them to retreat.
The bold commander followed them into   3195
The fortress, and it fell before his courage.
It was a short but brutal thing. The sword
Subdued them; by the sword the fort was lost.
The victors raged and grabbed the best as loot;
The vanquished trembled, hid, and were
    despoiled,   3200

113

And everywhere their groans and frightful
   mourning
Were mixed with fear and images of death.
Some ran into the mountains, and some swam
Into the lake; without their clothes and goods
They tried to flee. But those who wanted death   3205
Burned all the plunder, even their own houses.
Thus Iseo was destroyed by fire and sword,
And leaving nothing to the conquered people,
The royal army carried off rich treasure.
The king was thought to think the thoughts
   of God,   3210
And he was feared by every living being.

THE CITIZENS of Bergamo had gathered
So they might use their strength to take Volpino.
They marched with shining arms to make their
   camp
Beneath her gates and ramparts, and prepared   3215
To strike with greatest force and win the castle.
While some men hurled missiles, rocks, and fire,
Others worked at building catapults.
Without regard for life some tried to climb
The walls on ladders that were joined together,   3220
For every man had focused on their capture.
In several days the fear and lack of hope
That anyone would ever save the castle
(They saw on every side a ready army)
Forced their surrender of their sturdy ramparts,   3225
And quickly did those beaten sadly leave.
The town of Bergamo rejoiced because

This conquest wiped a blemish from their honor.
Confused and struck with fear, the Brescians
   mourned
And did not dare to leave their urban fortress.   3230
When the wheel begins to spin and fortune turns,
The high will trade their places with the low.

NOW BOLD MILAN was moved to savage war
And vexed the clients of the king. They blocked
Their castles and their citadels by siege.   3235
Between the city of Milan and Como
The noble castle of Carcano stood,
Protected by high ramparts and defenses.
Within its walls there dwelled a band of people,
Noble, strong, and terrible in war.   3240
They served the king alone and scorned Milan.
Now when our leader went, for reasons most
Compelling, to visit cities far away,
Milan attempted to subdue Carcano
And prepared to break that hostile race by war.   3245
Her army in high spirits built a camp
And continued day and night to press by siege
And storm the men enclosed within her walls.
These steadily protected the defenses
And rushed their legates to the friendly monarch,   3250
From whom they asked for help. At once the king
Collected troops and ordered his best vassals
To hasten to their aid with banners flying.
When Milan had learned fierce Frederick was
   approaching
And was ready for a fight, she hesitated;   3255

Could she by flight avoid the risk of battle,
Or better, face the royal standards armed,
Standing firm until the matter's settled?
While shame was urging this and terror that,
The king approached, as they considered
    options, 3260
And with them all surrounded Frederick cut
The road on which they came and went to home,
Like insects in a military column
That carry bits of food back to their nest.
The multitude enclosed in narrow confines 3265
Was terrified because they feared to fight
The sovereign of the empire and their lord,
Whom they could not escape. Then came Oberto,
A bishop and a lover of his people,
Who was in camp and gave this rousing speech: 3270
"O citizens, whose brilliant feats resound
Throughout the world, recall the grace and virtue
Of your fathers. Show your strength, I pray,
And when the time is right, demand a battle.
The missiles of this savage king surround us, 3275
And no one can depart except by force.
Therefore, my heroes, ready arms and spirits,
And clear a path with swords. Provide for your
Salvation and defend your country's borders.
Don't hesitate and victory will be ours. 3280
You fight for neither plunder nor for power,
But for justice and protection of the Church,
Your mother, for whose rights you took up arms.
Oh let the fear of black death disappear!
But raise your brilliant minds to hope and trust. 3285

God favors those who have the better cause,
And if by chance you lose your life in battle,
Then heaven will become your home forever."
Excited by this speech, the people burned
With love for Mars. They'd test their fortune
    now.   3290
Thus soon they broke from camp and charged
    their foes.
A trumpet raised a frightful din that shook
The clouds, and boldly did they rush with great
Commotion. The royal column also ran
To fight with frightful shouts and weapons
    raised.   3295
Helmets gleamed and shields crashed as the
    knights in battle
Clashed. Behind them foot with banners dashed.
They fought with bows. They fought with rocks,
    with swords
Or throwing spears. They fought with all their
    might.
Like hail upon the roof the blows resounded   3300
On their shields, and limbs were bathed
    with sweat.
They traded wounds and men died by the
    hundreds
In the clamor and the tumult of that battle.
The cloud of dust had turned the air to black,
Through which the king in golden armor
    gleamed,   3305
And on his stallion he led bands of vassals.

His naked sword struck those he found before him
And like a hungry lion he attacked.

IT WAS the custom that the high carroccio
Would fly the banner of the Milanese.   3310
A team of oxen harnessed for a cart
Pulled this wagon as they marched to war.
The standard was protected like a fortress
By youths and troops who bound themselves
    by oath
To guard and not desert their shining banner.   3315
It was to there they fled, if fortune turned,
To stand and fight with all their strength,
    and there
They could attack and break the hostile column.
When Frederick saw the banner on this wagon,
Defended by an army of his foes,   3320
He raged and rushed it with his sword and spear.
The soldier with his heart aflame destroyed it.
With his hard blade he raved and smashed this
    wagon
And then exulted, while proclaiming triumph.
The dead were everywhere for he spared no one.   3325
Behold, he hears his allies over there
Are broken and are fleeing, for the woods
And hilly nature of the place had blocked
His view. Then like a torrent or a storm
The fierce commander slaughtered with his
    sword   3330
And left the field littered with his victims.

BOOK FIVE

THE MEN from Bergamo collected all
Their strength and followed him who triumphed in
His shining armor. The troops, desiring to
Protect him, traded wounds audaciously.   3335
Some died with arms in hand (their bodies
   broken),
And some were captured near their lifeless horses.
It was a slaughter. Later, after battle,
He sought his tents with limbs that dripped
   with blood.
When he prepared again to risk a fight,   3340
A crowd of trembling vassals rushed to him.
They asked if he would leave this camp with them,
Since he saw his savage cohorts turn their backs.

HERE END THE EXPLOITS OF
EMPEROR FREDERICK BARBAROSSA
IN LOMBARDY AND ITALY.

NOTES TO THE TEXT

Book One

Line 8. "The colony of the Romans, once called Farther Italy, was separated into three provinces: Venetia, Aemilia, and Liguria. Aquileia was the metropolis of the first, Ravenna of the second, and Milan of the third." Mierow, p. 126 (2:13).

11. "The 'consular commune' was the commune in its first stage of development, so called because it was governed by officials known as 'consuls.'... The consulate, the assembled body of consuls, was the commune's highest executive and judicial magistracy. All important daily matters were discussed and decided here." Lauro Martines, *Power and Imagination, City-States in Renaissance Italy* (New York: Vintage Books, 1980), pp. 23, 27; and Waley, pp. 60-61. In the second section (pp. xxxvii-cii) of his introduction to *Gli atti del comune di Milano fino all'anno MCCXVI* (Milan: Capriolo & Massimino, 1919), Cesare Manaresi has a description of Milan's *organi del comune.*

17. "Milan ravaged Lodi in 1111 and Como in 1127; their conflicts involved traffic rights on the Po and Lambro rivers." Martines, p. 23. These victories offered an opportunity for great commercial expansion because they presented the possibility of joining the Alpine passes with the Po. Gian Luigi Barni, "La Lotta contro il Barbarossa," in vol. 4 of *Storia di Milano.* Ed. G. Martini (Milan: Fondazione Treccani degli Alfieri, 1954), p. 7.

20. "The inhabitants [of Lodi] were scattered amongst six open villages, and the market which had brought riches to them was done away with. For forty-seven years Lodi disappears from the list

of Lombard cities; during this period her citizens groaned under the harsh rule of their rivals." Butler, p. 76.

41. Pavia was seen as Milan's main obstacle in Lombardy. Barni, p. 7. See also Martines, p. 22; and Butler, pp. 56-57.

55-56. Frederick was elected in Frankfurt on March 4, 1152.

57. This line is close to Vergil's description of Aeneas (*Aen*. 1.545), and it is probably meant to designate Frederick as the new Aeneas. "In Aeneas, then, moral virtue (*iustitia, pietas*) takes the place of 'wisdom' and coexists, apparently without conflict, with his abilities as a fighter. He is (6.403) '...*Pietate insignis et armis,*' and in such cases his *pietas* is always mentioned first." Curtius, p. 173. See above p. xxxii.

75. "This was at about the beginning of the month of October, almost two years having elapsed since the expedition had first been vowed." Mierow, p. 124 (2:11). This is a good example of mannerist circumlocution.

78. The number may well be too high. Frederick in his letter to Otto of Freising spoke of 1,800 soldiers (Mierow, p. 20). The word *miles* (soldier) is ambiguous. About the use of *miles* in another passage, Mierow wrote (p. 18): "Like other twelfth-century writers, Otto uses *miles* in more than one sense. It may mean the army as a unit, or a soldier irrespective of class. In the present instance, the *miles* is clearly the heavy-armed cavalryman – the free vassal of noble blood – as opposed to the sergeant...." Our poet called the 4,000 who accompanied the king *proceres*, which has many definitions including great men of the realm and vassals. Citing Dettloff, Simonsfeld (p. 244) believed the total number was 6,000.

81. Frederick probably did make a short stop at Verona after crossing the Alps, but the events immediately following, according to Otto of Freising (Mierow, p. 124 [2:11]) and Otto Morena (p. 12),

took place at Roncaglia some days later. Roncaglia is a plain about three miles from Piacenza.

93. Although the speech is in the poet's own words, Schmale-Ott believes that, like all the other speeches, it may conform to what was actually spoken. Schmale-Ott, p. 4 n. 6. According to Otto of Freising, two consuls, Oberto dall' Orto and Gerardo Negri, defended Milan. Mierow, p. 130 (2:16). Oberto was a famous jurist. See Adolf Hofmeister, "Eine neue Quelle zur Geschichte Friedrich Barbarossas, *De ruina civitatis Terdonae,*" *Neues Archiv der Gesellschaft für ältere deutsche Geschichteskunde* 43 (1922): 97.

182. Otto Morena (p. 13) puts the bribe at 4,000 silver marks. It was first offered at Roncaglia.

209. The place is Monza. Moitia is a form not otherwise found, and Schmale-Ott believed it to be probably a scribal error. Schmale-Ott, p. 8 n. 2.

210-15. "The only royal coronation that until then had taken place in Monza was the one of anti-king Conrad (1128), and it was held in the church of St. Michael, while only the accompanying Mass was celebrated at St. John's. Moreover Pavia, not Monza, was the traditional place of coronation. The tradition regarding Monza, obviously Milanese in origin, was apparently consciously constructed because of the events of 1128. It can be traced back with certainly only to that year." (My translation.) Schmale-Ott, p. 8 n. 3. In fact Frederick was crowned in Pavia on April 17, 1155.

266-68. The land was ravaged during Milan's recent war with Pavia. Testa, p. 130.

269. "As we there demanded a market of them and they refused to furnish it, we caused to be taken and destroyed by fire their finest fortress, Rosate, which held five hundred men." Mierow, Fred. Letter to Otto, p. 18. In a preliminary draft that the Lombard League

advanced in 1175 as a basis for peace negotiations with Frederick, emperors on their coronation journey to Rome had the right to an untroubled passage and to the possibility to supply themselves adequately at a market. Appelt, p. 97.

271-72. Trecate is east of Novara, and Galleate northwest of Trecate. For the sequence of events, see Schmale-Ott, p. 10 n. 5.

317. This incident is probably dramatized. According to Hofmeister (p. 102), this line refers to the usual change of officials that took place at the beginning of the year. No consul was reelected, but among the new consuls there was Anselm de Orto, a son of one of the old ones and a famous legal writer like his father. The exact number of consuls is not known with certainty, and it probably varied from year to year. Manaresi (p. xliii) suggests that twelve was the usual number in the second half of the twelfth century.

337. Pavia paid Frederick to destroy Tortona, but it was in his interest to do so. By attacking her, he could cut Milan's road to the port of Genoa. Barni, p. 5.

381-83. The ancient stone seems to be only a Vergilian allusion (*Aen.* 8.478). Otto of Freising said that it was made of brick, but he puts its origin at the time of Tarquin the Proud. Mierow, p. 133 (2:20).

393. The direction of the defense was probably in the hands of the Milanese garrison and the Margrave Malaspina. Hofmeister, p. 103.

396-97. "After this the king, desiring to vanquish nature by nature's aid, that is, to constrain by lack of drinking water those who were hedged in by nature's defenses, proceeded to make the aforesaid spring useless for human needs. There were thrown into it the rotting and putrid corpses of men and beasts. But not even thus could the pitiful thirst of the townsmen be restrained. Another device was found. Burning torches, with flames of sulphur and pitch, were cast into the aforesaid spring, and thus the waters themselves were made bitter and useless for human needs." Mierow, p. 136 (2:21). There may have been a shortage of food as well. See Hofmeister, p. 117.

403. "The poet does not speak of the first attempt at negotiations by Tortona's clergy. (See Hofmeister, *De ruina* [c. 8] pp. 153-54; Otto of Freising, *Gesta*, 2:24ff. In Otto's version in contrast to *De ruina* the clergy ask only for themselves.) The final negotiations, which led to the surrender of the city, came about through the mediation of Abbot Bruno of Chiaravalle." (My translation.) Schmale-Ott, p. 15 n. 1.

426. Actually the siege lasted just a little over two months from February 13, until April 18, 1155. Barni, p. 15.

451. Mierow's observation (p. 142 n. 53) on Otto of Freising's treatment of these events applies equally to this version. "Though Otto does his best to make Frederick's campaign seem successful, it is clear that essentially the attempt to reduce Lombardy had utterly failed. The very choice of Tortona rather than Milan as an example to the Lombard towns was a confession of imperial weakness. The reduction of Tortona enabled Frederick to turn southward without complete loss of face, but he left in his rear a Milan untouched, powerful, and in full opposition. Nor could he well afford the two months lost at Tortona; time will not now permit him to settle accounts with the Normans on this expedition. Perhaps only William of Sicily gained by this siege."

456-58. Frederick arrived in the neighborhood of Bologna on May 13 and celebrated Pentecost there.

460. Guido di Ranieri di Sasso was rector and *podestà* of Bologna from 1151 to 1154.

490-91. The scholars were held liable for the debts of their fellow countrymen.

496-99. "When one of the professors complained that Bolognese students were oppressed by unjust debts, Frederick issued the law *Habita,* which extended imperial protection to professors of law and also, with certain immunities as well, to students of law. Further, it placed each student under the jurisdiction either of the local bishop or (a simultaneously alluring and sobering prospect!) of his professor." Benson, p. 363. See also n. 114 on that page. This is the first mention of that law, which was first promulgated here. See also Kurt Zeillinger, "Das erste roncaglische Lehensgesetz Friedrich Barbarossas, Das Scholarenprivileg *(Authentica Habita)* und Gottfried von Viterbo," *Römische Historische Mitteilungen* 26 (1984): 204.

580. Towns were difficult to eradicate because many burghers held property in the country. Munz (pp. 153-54) writes: "This unusual feature of Lombard city life aided the undoing of Frederick. For it meant that his policy of destroying towns when they proved too defiant was ultimately completely unsuccessful. True, when a city was razed to the ground there was much lamentation; but the citizens simply dispersed in the countryside and probably found shelter in the farms and manors. When Frederick's army departed, they came out again and started to rebuild. And since the buildings in the city were for the most part fairly primitive ones, the rebuilding was neither too onerous nor too laborious. In this way, any direct retaliation against a city proved rather fruitless." This may be true, but the author of the *De ruina* said that Tortona was rebuilt on a smaller scale. Hofmeister, pp. 98-100.

BOOK TWO

Line 614. Mount Joy was the medieval name for the Monte Mario, a hill in the environs of Rome that would have offered an impressive view of the old city to arriving pilgrims. Otto of Freising (Mierow, pp. 144-45 [2:29]) stated that the Roman representatives met Frederick between Rome and Sutri, but Frederick's letter to Otto placed the meeting at Rome.

620-29. "The conditions were these: that he should abandon the cause of the Pope, and help them to put an end to his dominion in Rome, which should again be governed as a republic; that he should respect their laws and customs and protect them from the license of his soldiers; and finally, that he should pay the senators, who would crown him in the Capitol, five thousand pounds of silver." Testa, p. 142.

631-32. Frederick may be astonished but he is not so confused as to break good rhetorical form. He begins his speech with a *captatio benevolentiae,* a type of introduction that is to make the hearer favorably disposed to what comes next.

637. There was a custom that the emperor swear an oath, but the demand for a money payment was extraordinary. It had been traditional since the time of Gregory VII for the city to request money from the popes on their accession, "and they may have simply felt that if Adrian had not been able to pay, Frederick ought to...." Munz, p. 84 n. 1.

644. Because of the desecration of St. Peter's in 846 by Moslem raiders, Pope Leo IV built fortifications around the Vatican. This area became known as the Leonine City. There is some dispute as to the gate by which Frederick entered. Following Otto of Freising (Mierow, p. 150 [2:32]), Holtzmann (p. 263) said it was the Golden Gate in the area of the present Porta Angelica. Schmale-Ott (p. 22 n. 6) agreed and stated that it was the customary royal entrance to the city. But Ullmann maintained "that he entered the Leonine city with his German entourage from his stopping place outside Rome not through the Porta Collina near the Castle of Angelo, but through the Porta Viridaria which was, so to speak, the back entrance to St. Peter's." Walter Ullmann, "The Pontificate of Adrian IV," *The Cambridge Historical Journal* 11 (1955): 241.

657. Nicholas Breakspeare took the name of Adrian IV (1154-59), and he was the only English pope.

659-60. Actually the pope had traveled to Rome with Frederick, and he had returned to St. Peter's only a few hours earlier. Adrian's chief advisor, Cardinal Octavian, led a large part of the imperial army into the city through a small gate between St. Peter's and the Castel Sant' Angelo the night before and secured the area around the basilica. Giesebrecht, *Kaiserzeit*, 5:62.

662-64. According to Ullmann (pp. 240-43) the coronation was something of a triumph for the papacy in its struggle with the empire. Contrary to custom, Frederick was anointed before, not during, Mass and at a side altar, not at the main one, because Adrian wanted to emphasize that the coronation of an emperor was not a sacrament. Munz (p. 85) disputed Ullmann's thesis, but anyway the crowning, not the anointing, was the part of the ceremony emphasized in the twelfth century, as our poet attests.

672-79. In order to avoid conflict Frederick had arrived at St. Peter's at an unexpected time, early in the morning on Saturday. Since Sunday was the usual coronation day, it took some time for the Romans to realize what happened and to react. Giesebrecht, *Kaiserzeit*, 5:62.

707. Henry the Lion was duke of Saxony and Bavaria; and as head of the Guelphs he was potentially Frederick's most powerful adversary among the German lords. Henry and his men may have been responsible for the imperial success in this battle. Gregorovius, 4,2:543 n.1.

717. He was count of Martinengo from the house of the counts of Bergamo. According to Holtzmann (p. 278) and Gundlach (3:264), he may have been the source of this account of Frederick's trip to Rome.

806-7. There is no clear information about Arnold's role in Brescia and Milan.

811-15. Arnold, perhaps a student of Abelard, advocated radical reform of the Church, but his proposals were condemned by the Second Lateran Council in 1139. After his expulsion from Italy, he went to France and helped in Abelard's defense at the Council of Sens, where both were condemned. In 1141 he was expelled from France at the behest of Bernard of Clairvaux. Around 1145 he was reconciled to the Church but was excommunicated by Eugenius III in 1148. See Frugoni.

901-7. While in Rome Frederick received a group of southern Italian nobles who had risen in rebellion against William I of Sicily. Frederick gave his support and sent an embassy led by Count Guido Guerra to Apulia. It was believed that an imperial army would soon follow. But on their return journey the count and his companions were seized. Spoleto was also assessed a *foedrum* of 800 pounds, but it paid only a part of that sum and used counterfeit money to do so. Giesebrecht, *Kaiserzeit*, 5:66-68.

968. Frederick received the embassy at Spoleto.

976-99. The Brusati were a Brescian family and the lords of Volpino. They were related by marriage to the Mozzi, a family from Bergamo. An account of the dispute between Giovanni Brusati and Gislinzone Mozzi can be found in Belotti, 1:340.

995-1001. Although there is no clear evidence, Brescia's reluctance to purchase these castles may have been caused by their desire not to offend their bishop. The Brusati held Volpino from him, and he was the lord for these castles as well. This dispute then turned around a legal point about the right to alienate fiefs. Although there is no mention of it in the poem, Frederick issued laws at Roncaglia in both 1154 and in 1158 to prevent sale of a fief without the overlord's permission. Brusati's sale to Bergamo took place around 1126. Ibid.

1033. "Turning from there toward Ancona, we encountered Palaeologus, the most noble prince of the Greeks, and Maroducas, his associate, with other envoys of [the emperor of] Constantinople. They solemnly promised to give us an enormous sum of money to induce us to go into Apulia and undertake by our mighty power the destruction of William, the enemy of both empires. But because our army had been too greatly weakened by its many hardships and campaigns, our leaders decided to return home rather than descend into Apulia." Mierow, Fred. Letter to Otto, p. 20. Notice the marriage is not mentioned in this account because our poet was in error about the time of its negotiation, which took place in September of 1153.

1046. The poet is in error. This event took place at the Chiusa di Verona, a pass about ten miles northwest of Verona.

1085-87. The king crossed the Brenner in the middle of September 1155. He had accomplished little in his year in Italy. For an assessment of this first trip see Giesebrecht, *Kaiserzeit,* 5:72-73. According to Otto of Freising (Mierow, pp. 160-61 [2:43]) there were many disturbances in Germany during his absence, and perhaps the people saw the emperor as a restorer of peace.

1109. Rainald III of Upper Burgundy. "Frederick extended his influence in Burgundy by marrying the sixteen-year-old Beatrix in 1156, heiress to substantial possessions in upper Burgundy and in Provence." Fuhrmann, p. 150.

1110-14. Although there is obviously rhetorical exaggeration in this passage, Beatrice was an impressive woman. "Frederick's Burgundian wife Beatrix certainly played a large part in turning the itinerant Staufer court into a centre of chivalric culture. Beatrix had literary tastes, and in the course of her thirty years of married life (she died in her early forties) evidently took an active part in the cultural life of court, which she generally accompanied even on the exhausting Italian expeditions. Barbarossa allowed her free reign, so that he came to acquire the reputation of being a man under his wife's thumb, a *vir uxoratus.*" Fuhrmann, p. 179. Beatrice had at least ten children, eight of whom were sons.

1130. The castle of Palosco was southeast of Bergamo and in its territory.

1134-36. The Brescians kept their military preparations secret, and Belotti speculates (1:342) that Cremona would have sent help if she had been prepared.

1138. The field of combat was known as Grumore. Ibid.

1159. It was the night of Saturday, March 10, 1156. Ibid.

1204. This number might be too low. A Brescian chronicle recorded 2,500 dead and as many captured, but it too is probably an exaggeration. Schmale-Ott, p. 40 n. 10.

1226. Gerard de Berneto was one of the consuls for 1156.

1235. The great banner of Bergamo was solemnly displayed in Brescia on the anniversary of the battle in the church of SS. Faustinus and Giovita. Butler, p. 106. Monaci gives the text of a contemporary poem celebrating Brescia's victory. Monaci, *Gesta di Federico I,* p. 49.

1244. Lanfred of Pontecarale was from a noble family and was often mentioned in the documents from that time.

1274-77. Belotti maintains (1:344) that Bergamo was in no condition to continue the war after that defeat.

1278. He was abbot of San Sepolcro della Valle d'Astino.

1313-15. It is around this time that the famous oath of a thousand Bergamasks was made. In order that the peace be solemnly observed, a thousand citizens were selected from the city and the suburbs among the various classes and made to swear. Belotti, 1:344.

It was not uncommon for large numbers of citizens to take such oaths. There is a later example of an oath of a thousand citizens, which the Pisans took in making a treaty with Genoa in 1188. Ferdinand Opll, *Stadt und Reich im 12. Jahrhundert (1125-1190)* (Vienna: Hermann Böhlaus, 1986), p. 206 n. 14.

BOOK THREE

Line 1335. Gerardus was bishop of Bergamo from 1146 to 1167. He was one of the ecclesiastics who took part in the emperor's wedding to Beatrice of Burgundy, and Barbarossa had heaped many honors upon him. He was one of the few Italian bishops who supported Frederick in the schism that arose after the death of Adrian IV. See Belotti, 1:347-48; and Pesenti, pp. 65-67.

1401. Obizo Bucafel was one of the consuls from Pavia. This meeting may have taken place at a diet held in Fulda, where it was decided to war upon Milan.

1403. Albericus de Merlino was bishop of Lodi from 1158 to 1168.

1405. He was bishop of Como from 1125 to 1158. He also represented Como to the emperor in 1153.

1437. This is a variation of a rhetorical technique known as the brevity formula. Of course it is not a means of being brief but rather of demonstrating to the audience that the speaker knows the rules of rhetoric, that he is the eloquent Obzibo. See Curtius, p. 487.

1447. Como conquered the island in 1169.

1449. Lisna may have been a small castle in the neighborhood of Bergamo. See Schmale-Ott (p. 48 n.5) for a discussion of the problem raised by this name.

1504. In Worms at Easter time the princes took a oath against Milan.

1559-60. The troops were to have mustered on the vigil of Pentecost.

1589-1614. The disintegration of the Polish kingdom gave Frederick an opportunity to expand his influence. Boleslaw III left four sons, among whom he divided his kingdom. Each received an independent principality. To the eldest he left the title of duke and the capital, Krakow. Yet he did so with the stipulation that the title would not necessarily devolve on his children, but on the oldest in the entire dynasty. It was a recipe for disaster. Shortly after their father's death in 1138 the younger brothers joined forces against the eldest, Vladislav, and expelled him. Since he was married to a niece of Conrad III, he sought refuge at the imperial court, but Conrad's attempts to restore him were ineffectual. According to Rahewin (Mierow, p. 176 [3:2]) the Poles also ceased giving fealty and paying a tribute of 500 marks each year. Frederick, however, took the opportunity to reassert imperial power over Boleslaw IV, the brother who took Vladislav's throne. Among the conditions that Frederick imposed on him was the obligation to participate in the Italian campaign. Although the duke reneged on this, the Polish expedition was something of a high-water mark in imperial relations with that country. Perhaps that is why the poet tries, although not very successfully, to describe it. The Polish historian Oscar Halecki writes: "The second son of Boleslas III, who bore his father's name, could not defend himself as well as his predecessors in similar circumstances, and was obliged to humiliate himself as no other Polish prince had done before the Emperor. It is true that he was able to keep the supreme power in Poland, but on conditions which clearly demonstrated the imperial suzerainty." Oscar Halecki, *A History of Poland*, 9th ed. (New York: David McKay, 1976), p. 25.

1649-1733. The defenders of Vigevano, who were led by the Margrave of Montferrat, decided to risk an open battle because the fort was too poorly provisioned to withstand a long siege. The battle and siege took place in June of 1157. Testa, p. 166.

1653. According to Otto of Freising (Mierow, p. 129 [2:15]) the Margrave of Montferrat was the only northern Italian noble who was not under the jurisdiction of a commune. His power base was mainly in Piedmont, and he was a strong imperial supporter. William the Old (1135-90), so called because of his prematurely gray hair, was an uncle by marriage to Barbarossa. Usseglio, 1:136.

1690. This is one of the few times that the poet became personal.

1708. "The Consuls, in planning and executing this undertaking, are said to have availed themselves of the advice of Maestro Guglielmo Guintellino, who in architecture and in making engines of war excelled everyone else in Lombardy.... By him is said to have been designed and built that bridge over the Ticino between Abbiate and Capoli, than which no finer one had as yet been seen in Lombardy. And now, amidst the preparations for this war, he invented a new kind of scythe-armed chariot, and made a very powerful catapult." Testa, p. 153. Barni (p. 23 n. 1) is more cautious: "Of this master Guintelmo or Guintellino we now know very little except that he was in the service of Milan from 1156 to 1162." (My translation.) See also Hyde, p. 76.

1730. The castle surrendered after a three-day siege. Milan's success here and the threat she now posed to Pavia may have accelerated Frederick's return to Italy. Barni, p. 26.

1785-93. Rahewin's description of this muster is similar to that of the poet. Mierow, p. 201 (3:26).

1790. "Perhaps the most striking example of Frederick's exalted conception of the imperial authority was when, in 1158, he raised Duke Vladislav II of Bohemia to the rank of king. The novelty lay not in the Emperor's claims over Bohemia, nor in the notion that he could receive the allegiance and fealty of a king (for that was not unusual), but in the idea that he could create a king where previously there had been no kingdom, for kings were normally thought to receive their power from God, through the hands of the clergy." R. H. C. Davis, *A History of Medieval Europe from Constantine to St. Louis,* 2d ed. (London: Longman, 1987), p. 311.

1802. The force was gathered on June 8.

1828-31. "To secure the safety of the suburbs which had sprung up outside the original circuit of the walls, they constructed the large moat, or rather canal, which, under the name Naviglio Grande, forms such a picturesque feature in the modern city. This moat, circular in form, formed the boundary of the city for centuries afterwards. On the inner side ramparts were erected, with gates of stone. It is said that on this work they spent the immense sum of fifty thousand marks of silver, eleven hundred thousand pounds of our money." Butler, p. 105.

1837. Lomello, west of Pavia, was rebuilt by Milan.

1842. Maleo was rebuilt at about the same time. It is west of Cremona on the Adda.

1860-61. Around the end of June in 1158, Frederick crossed the Brenner Pass, and in early July he was at Verona.

1872-99. Barni (p. 29) surmises that this speech preserved a *"valore spirituale"* that existed in the city at the time, and even Frederick himself might have felt it.

2032. The emperor was in the territory of Brescia for about fifteen days, according to Otto Morena (p. 47). Brescia saved herself by "giving up sixty hostages and no small sum of money." Mierow, p. 202 (3:27).

BOOK FOUR

Line 2078. The sources are in dispute as to whether any of the bridges over the Adda were left standing by the Milanese. Giesebrecht (*Kaiserzeit*, 5:155) resolved the situation by postulating that all bridges were destroyed with the exception of the one at Cassano.

2084. Vaprio and Cropello are in the neighborhood of Cassano on the Adda.

2098-2114. According to Giesebrecht (*Kaiserzeit*, 5:155) three impetuous Bohemian knights tried to ford the river, and two of them made it. This inspired the king of Bohemia to try a crossing. A Lombard prisoner is said to have taken him to a shallow spot at Corneliano, where the king leaped on his horse and crossed over with his knights. Yet the sources are not in agreement as to whether in fact the emperor took the initiative for the crossing or whether it was the king of Bohemia and Conrad of Dachau. See Schmale-Ott, p. 69 n. 8.

2114-29. The poet is here compressing events to the point of distortion. On the day after the crossing, with the bridge still in enemy hands, Vladislav learned that Milanese troops were approaching. Royal troops, who were sent to scout, engaged them in combat and defeated them at Gorgonzola, a place west of Cassano, which now is famous for blue cheese. This victory meant that the bridge had to be abandoned or its defenders would be encircled. Barni, p. 30.

2142-51. The siege began on July 25 and lasted no more than a few days. According to Barni (p. 30), Trezzo defended another bridge and threatened the flank of the imperial army.

2215. The siege of Milan began on August 6. For Frederick's activity in the meantime, see Giesebrecht, *Kaiserzeit*, 5:156-57.

2267. "The *Brolo* was a large grass field, shaded with trees. Pavia, Tortona, and other cities of Italy had also their Broli. The place, open to the public, belonged until the fourteenth century, to the Archbishop. The citizens used to come there to take their pleasure, to practice warlike exercises, and to transact their affairs. It served also for the public markets, the most important of which was held in it on Fridays; and in time churches, hospitals, and other public buildings were erected in it." Testa, p. 152 n. 1.

2268. This is the famous tent given to Frederick by Henry II of England. "Among these gifts we beheld a tent, very large in extent and of the finest quality. If you ask its size, it could not be raised except by machinery and a special sort of instrument and props; if you ask its quality, I should imagine that neither in material nor in workmanship will it ever be surpassed by any equipment of this kind." Mierow, pp. 178-79 (3:7).

2276. Giesebrecht (*Kaiserzeit*, 5:161) estimated Frederick's army at 100,000 men, 15,000 of whom were knights.

2303-4. Rome also sent a contingent under the command of the city prefect Peter. Yet even this large army could not completely close off the city, which remained open especially in the west and north. Giesebrecht, *Kaiserzeit*, 5:161.

2311-30. The accounts of the Milanese sally differ from source to source. It may be that there were several of them, but it is now impossible to sort them out. Schmale-Ott, p. 76 n. 4.

2312. The Porta Romana was the chief gate of the city.

2386. "At the distance of not more than an arrow's flight from the Roman Gate of the Ditch, was a quadrangular tower, so high that it commanded the battlements of that gate. It had for its base four massive pillars, from which sprang four great arches, upon which it rested. It is said that it was originally one of those porticoes called

Arches of Janus, which in Rome and in its colonies used to be built in the marketplaces, for the accommodation of those who bought and sold there. But by some it is thought to have been a triumphant arch, erected for the ornament, or in remembrance of some ancient victory.... It had obtained the name of the Roman Arch, no doubt, from the current tradition that it was a work of the Romans, a tradition confirmed by the solidity and great size of its squared stones, which were wrought and joined with such wonderful skill, that nothing could be seen of the mortar which fastened them together but the very finest line. Forty men, with their arms and provisions, could be conveniently stationed there, and so many had been sent by the Milanese Consuls for the defence of this ante-mural fortress." Testa, pp. 195-96. Archaeology confirmed the size and position of the arch. Barni, p. 33 n. 8.

2509-10. See above, p. xxxii.

2535-47. Frederick's terms to Milan can be found in Rahewin. Mierow, pp. 220-23 (3:47).

2592. "And on being asked by the Emperor what place in the neighbourhood would suit them best, they named Monteghezonne, a rising ground upon the Adda, four miles from old Lodi." Testa, p. 190. Munz (p. 161) added that new Lodi was a "veritable fortified capital," a center of operations and imperial residence in Lombardy. Our poet erroneously followed Rahewin in placing the foundation of New Lodi before the diet of Roncaglia. See Holtzmann, p. 275.

2619-21. According to Otto Morena (p. 63), Frederick first issued the command against Piacenza in January of 1159.

2630-78. Munz (p. 171) saw "a general feeling of disquiet arise in various cities over the way in which Frederick was implementing the Roncaglia decree." An anti-imperial riot in Milan did not originate from a specific grievance but from "a growing general resistance to imperial policies in general" (p. 174). Fear and mistrust were in the air. To some extent the medieval poet then mirrors the modern historian by placing the source of the discord in the temptations of Allecto, i.e., in the psychological state of Milan and her allies.

2733-35. Lothar unsuccessfully besieged Crema in 1132.

BOOK FIVE

Line 2773-88. Frederick was not in Emilia, but rather he resided in Piedmont until the beginning of January 1159. The embassy departed from Occimiano, which is between Alessandria and Casale. See Holtzmann, p. 275. According to Rahewin, (Mierow, p. 260 [4:23]), Rainald von Dassel, Count Palatinate Otto von Wittelsbach, and Count Gozwin von Heinsberg were sent, but the Milanese *Gesta* (p. 35) and Otto Morena (p. 64) mention only the first two. According to Giesebrecht's version (*Kaiserzeit*, 5:187), only Rainald and Otto went into the inner city, for the other representatives took their lodging in the suburbs. Eventually because of threats from a mob, the entire embassy with the exception of Rainald fled in the middle of a night. Rainald departed the next morning seemingly on good terms with the Milanese, but the incident aroused a deadly hate in his heart against Milan.

2811-26. Trezzo was the castle where Frederick had placed his treasury and many hostages. Testa, p. 220. It was important for control of the neighborhood and for access between Milan and Bergamo. Giesebrecht, *Kaiserzeit*, 5:170. See also the note to line 2142. It is unclear whether this Rudiger was the imperial chamberlain or a count from Florence.

2827. According to Giesebrecht (*Kaiserzeit*, 5:193), the siege began on April 11, the Saturday before Easter, but this date is not certain.

2868. The siege lasted three days, too short a period for Frederick to bring help, although he attempted to do so. Giesebrecht,

Kaiserzeit, 5:193. Munz (p. 177) considers this siege as "the straw that broke the camel's back." Frederick's patience was now exhausted, and Milan was now put under the ban of the empire.

2905-7. According to the Milanese *Gesta* (p. 36), there were 400 infantry men, some knights, and a consul named Manfred (Martin in other sources) de Dugniano.

2911. The siege began in the first week of July. "Crema was a small, but strong city, situated on the right bank of the Serio, in a low place, marshy in some parts because of the frequent overflowing of its river. Wide and deep ditches, full of water, with double walls, the outer one of great height, at that time surrounded it.... It was formerly subject to the Bishops of Cremona, but when the Commune of Cremona succeeded to the power of the Bishop, Crema withdrew itself, and joined the Milanese; and it had ever since continued faithful to them. Wherefore there had been now for several generations a deadly enmity between the Cremascans and the Cremonese; so that, even when they were not at open war, they would come, as if for sport, on Sundays and feast days, after the services and the wine, to confront one another on the banks of their river; and defiances, insults, arrows, and blows would be exchanged between them." Testa, p. 227. Frederick was offered 15,000 silver marks by Cremona to issue a command that Crema tear down her walls and fill her moat. Giesebrecht, *Kaiserzeit*, 5:186.

2915. The Ombriana gate, which is in the west.

2926-27. Frederick appeared around July 10.

2951. According to Giesebrecht (*Kaiserzeit*, 5:202-3) the empress and Henry the Lion arrived at Crema on July 20. The next day she went to Lodi where a festive greeting was prepared for her, but soon she left for a not easily identifiable place called Veruga. Later she appeared at San Bassano, not far from Crema.

2976-3030. "This unseemly episode is recounted by Otto Morena (pp. 79-81), who says nine of the prisoners were killed, the *Gesta di Federico in Italia* (Monaci, pp. 112-13), and the *Gesta Federici in Lombardia* (Schmale-Ott, pp. 37-38), which says Frederick so used about twenty captives, of whom seven were killed." Mierow, p. 286 n. 186. Only Rahewin mentioned children among the victims.

2988-93. The tower must have been very remarkable, for Otto Morena (p. 73) states its equal did not exist in the west *(...quod ex hac maris parte nec par nec simile unquam visum fuit.)* Five hundred people were needed to set it in motion. Giesebrecht, *Kaiserzeit,* 5:202.

3059. Marchesius was the most talented of the masters at Crema for the building of war machines. Giesebrecht notes how important architects and engineers, like Vintelmo and Marchesius, were to the military operations of that day. Frederick invested another of them, Tinto Mussa de Gatta, who may have built the great tower, with a county. When the siege was over, the emperor destroyed military devices worth more than 2,000 silver marks. Giesebrecht, *Kaiserzeit,* 5:204, 214.

3065. The emperor gave him an expensive garment and a horse that he bought only a little time before at a cost of twelve silver pounds. Giesebrecht, *Kaiserzeit,* 5:210.

3097-99. Frederick ordered Marchesius to build a wooden scaffold more than forty yards high, from which a wooden bridge could be slid. It was used in conjunction with the tower. Giesebrecht, *Kaiserzeit,* 5:210-11.

3137. Henry the Lion. The peace terms are in Rahewin (Mierow, pp. 306-8 [4:72]). Pilgrim, the bishop of Aquileia, was also present.

3142. This happened near the end of January.

3154-59. The account here is not accurate. From Crema, the emperor went to Lodi and then to Pavia. The Milanese *Gesta* (p. 40) places the destruction of Milan's fields in the middle of May.

3164-3211. Giesebrecht asserts that the poem provided the earliest record of the capture of Iseo, and it helped him date this event to July 28, 1160. Giesebrecht, *Neue Gedichte,* p. 288 n. 24.

3236-3343. Carcano was a fortress northwest of Milan, and it was a thorn in her side. The castle was in the hands of troops from Seprio and Martesana, who were loyal to Emperor Frederick. Near the end of July 1160, the Milanese sent men to occupy the area and besiege the fortress. Those in the castle called upon Frederick for help. He was at Vighezzolo near Cantu with 1,000 knights, auxiliaries from Pavia, Novara, and Como, and the Margrave of Montferrat. On August 8, the emperor made camp at Tessera and blocked the probable paths of reinforcement. He set up roadblocks and trenches in such a manner that he was able to turn the besiegers into the besieged. Fortunes varied during the ensuing battle that was fought on August 9. At Tessera Frederick drove the attacking Milanese troops from his camp and was able to capture the *carroccio,* the Milanese war wagon, which had overturned and from whose mast a golden cross was ripped. When the king returned to camp, he felt that he had carried the day. In fact, he later claimed the battle to be a victory. But in another part of the field, Milan had attacked the Margrave of Montferrat, who had contingents from Novara, Como, and Vercelli with him. Inflicting heavy casualties, the Milanese caused them to turn and to run. In fact, only a violent thunderstorm prevented them from assaulting Frederick's camp.

The emperor now found his position so precarious that he retreated first to Como and then for greater security to Baradello, a castle not far from Como, whose defenses he had strengthened in the previous year. He left behind the bulk of his tents and his prisoners of war. The Milanese therefore also claimed victory, but on

August 20, they gave up the siege for fear that Frederick might bring another army against them or attack Milan, which was left practically undefended. Around the beginning of September, the Milanese were again active in the region, and Carcano is said to have surrendered to them on September 10. It is in the midst of this episode that the poem abruptly ends. My account is taken largely from Giesebrecht (*Kaiserzeit*, 5:282-87), but Barni (pp. 53-56) and Testa (pp. 253-56) also provided some details.

3268-88. Known as an ardent enemy of the emperor, he was the archbishop of Milan and had accompanied the troops. Carcano was a fief of the church of Milan. See Barni, p. 54; Testa, p. 253.

BIBLIOGRAPHY

TEXT OF THE POEM

Monaci, Ernesto, ed. *Gesta di Federico I in Italia*. Fonti per la Storia d'Italia. Vol. 1. Rome: Forzani, 1887.

Querenghi, Francesco, trans. *Gesta di Federico I Barbarossa in Italia*. Bergamo, 1936. (First published in *Bergomum*, n.s. 8 & 9 [1934 & 1935].)

Schmale-Ott, Irene, ed. *Carmen de gestis Frederici I. imperatoris in Lombardia*. Monumenta Germaniae Historica. Scriptores rerum Germanicarum in usum scholarum. Vol. 62. Hanover: Hahn, 1965.

OTHER SOURCES

Antonucci, Giovanni. "Magister Johannes Asinus de Gandino." *Bergomum*, n.s. 7 (1933): 217-19.

—. "Un nuovo documento a Giovanni Asino." *Bergomum*, n.s. 9 (1935): 64-65.

—. "Documenti inediti su Giovanni Asino." *Bergomum*, n.s. 10 (1936): 41-45.

—. "Magister Johannes Asinus, Documenti inediti." *Bergomum*, n.s. 12 (1938): 32-41.

Archpoet. *Die Gedichte des Archipoeta*. Ed. H. Watenphul and H. Krefeld. Heidelberg: Carl Winter, 1958.

Bernardus Silvestris. *Commentary on the First Six Books of Virgil's Aeneid*. Trans. with notes and introduction by Earl G. Schreiber and Thomas E. Maresca. Lincoln: University of Nebraska Press, 1979.

Gunther. *Ligurinus.* Ed. Erwin Assmann. Monumenta Germaniae Historica. Scriptores rerum Germanicarum in usum scholarum. Vol. 63. Hanover: Hahn, 1987.

Holder-Egger, Oswald, ed. *Gesta Federici I. imperatoris in Lombardia auctore cive Mediolanensi.* Monumenta Germaniae Historica. Scriptores rerum Germanicarum in usum scholarum. Vol. 27. Hanover: Hahn,1892.

Jaffé, Philipp, ed. *Monumenta Corbeiensia. Bibliotheca Rerum Germanicarum.* Vol. 1. 1864. Reprint, Aalen: Scientia, 1964.

John of Salisbury. *The Early Letters (1153-1161). The Letters of John of Salisbury.* Ed. W. J. Millor and H. E. Butler. Revised by C. N. L. Brooke. Vol. 1. London: Thomas Nelson & Sons, 1955.

Lucan. *The Civil War.* Cambridge, MA: Loeb Classical Library, 1928.

Morena, Otto. *Das Geschichtswerk des Otto Morena und seiner Fortsetzer über die Taten Friedrichs I in der Lombardei.* Ed. F. Güterbock. Monumenta Germaniae Historica. Scriptores rerum Germanicarum. N.s. 7. Berlin: Weidmann, 1930.

Otto, Bishop of Freising, and Rahewin. *The Deeds of Frederick Barbarossa.* Trans. and ed. Charles C. Mierow with Richard Emery. New York: Columbia University Press, 1953.

—. *Gesta Frederici seu rectius cronica.* Ed. Franz-Josef Schmale. Ausgewählte Quellen zur deutschen Geschichte des Mittelalters. Vol. 17. Berlin: Deutscher Verlag der Wissenschaften, 1965.

Turoldus. *The Song of Roland. An Analytical Edition.* Trans. Gerard Brault. 2 vols. University Park: Pennsylvania State University Press, 1978.

Walter of Chatillon. *Moralisch-Satirische Gedichte Walters von Chatillon.* Ed. Karl Strecker. Heidelberg: Carl Winter, 1929.

144

BIBLIOGRAPHY

STUDIES

Alexander, Michael. *The Poetic Achievement of Ezra Pound.* Berkeley and Los Angeles: University of California Press, 1981.

Appelt, Heinrich. "Friedrich Barbarossa und die italienischen Kommunen." In *Friedrich Barbarossa.* Ed. Gunther Wolf. *Wege der Forschung,* vol. 390. Darmstadt: Wissenschaftliche Buchgesellschaft, 1975. (First published in *Mitteilungen des Instituts für österreichische Geschichtsforschung* 72 (1964): 311-25.

Baethgen, Friedrich. "Monumenta Germaniae Historica. Bericht für die Jahre 1943-1948." *Deutsches Archiv für Erforschung des Mittelalters* 8 (1950): 1-25.

—. "Monumenta Germaniae Historica. Bericht für das Jahr 1955/ 56." *Deutsches Archiv für Erforschung des Mittelalters* 14 (1958): 1-15.

Balzani, Ugo. *Early Chroniclers of Europe. Italy.* London: Society for Promoting Christian Knowledge, 1883.

Barni, Gian Luigi. "La Lotta contro il Barbarossa." In vol 4 of *Storia di Milano.* Ed. G. Martini. Milan: Fondazione Treccani degli Alfieri, 1954.

Barraclough, Geoffrey. *The Medieval Papacy.* London: Thames & Hudson, 1968.

—. *The Origins of Modern Germany.* Oxford: Basil Blackwell, 1947.

Becker, Dietrich. "Die Belagerung von Crema bei Rahewin, im *Ligurinus* und im *Carmen de gestis Frederici I. imperatoris in Lombardia.*" Ph.D. diss. Julius-Maximilian University at Würzburg, 1975.

Belotti, Bortolo. *Storia di Bergamo e dei Bergamaschi.* 7 vols. Bergamo: Poligrafiche Bolis, 1959.

Bethmann, Ludwig. "Nachrichten. *Monumenta Germaniae historica.* Sammlungen von Handschriften und Urkunden Italiens aus dem Jahre 1854." *Archiv der Gesellschaft für ältere deutsche Geschichtskunde* 12 (1874): 201-426.

Benson, Robert L. "Political *renovatio.* Two Models from Roman Antiquity." In *Renaissance and Renewal in the Twelfth Century.* Ed. Robert L. Benson and Giles Constable. Cambridge, MA: Harvard University Press, 1982, pp. 339-86.

Bloch, Marc. *Feudal Society.* Trans. L. A. Manyon. 2 vols. Chicago: University of Chicago Press, 1964.

Blumenthal, Ute-Renate. *The Investiture Controversy. Church and Monarchy from the Ninth to the Twelfth Century.* Philadelphia: University of Pennsylvania Press, 1988.

Brackmann, Albert. "The Beginnings of the National State in Mediaeval Germany and the Norman Monarchies." In vol. 2 of *Mediaeval Germany 911-1250. Essays by German Historians.* Trans. and ed. Geoffrey Barraclough. New York: Barnes & Noble, 1938, pp. 281-300.

Bulst, Walther. "Politische und Hofdichtung der Deutschen bis zum hohen Mittelalter." *Deutsche Vierteljahrsschrift für Literaturwissenschaft und Geistesgeschichte* 15 (1937): 189-202.

Bumke, Joachim. *Mäzene im Mittelalter. Die Gönner und Auftraggeber der höfischen Literatur in Deutschland 1150-1300.* Munich: C. H. Beck'sche Verlags-buchhandlung, 1979.

Burdach, Konrad. *Walther von der Vogelweide. Philologische und historische Forshungen.* Leipzig: Duncker & Humblot, 1900.

Butler, W. F. *The Lombard Communes.* 1906. Reprint, New York: Haskell House, 1969.

Capasso, C. "Guelfi e Ghibellini a Bergamo." *Bergomum* 15,3 (1921): 1-44.

Chiodi, Luigi. "Gli inizi del comune di Bergamo. Note e appunti." *Bergomum,* n.s. 41 (1967): 1-29.

Chiri, Giuseppe. *La poesia epico-storica latina dell' Italia medioevale.* Istituto di Filologia Romanza della R. Università di Roma. Studi e Testi. Modena: Società Tipografica Modense, 1939.

BIBLIOGRAPHY

Collingwood, R. G. *The Idea of History*. 1946. Reprint, London: Oxford University Press, 1980.

Collins, S. T. *"De gestorum Frederici I* Codice Vaticano." *Annali della Scuola Normale Superiore di Pisa*, ser. 2, 20 (1951): 98-103.

Cremaschi, Giovanni. *Mosè del Brolo e la cultura a Bergamo nei secoli xi e xii.* Bergamo: Società Editrice S. Alessandro, 1945.

—. "Nuovo contributo alla biografia di Mosè del Brolo." *Bergomum*, n.s. 28 (1954): 49-58.

Curtius, Ernst Robert. *European Literature and the Latin Middle Ages*. Trans. Willard R. Trask. Princeton: Princeton University Press, 1953.

Davis, R. H. C. *A History of Medieval Europe from Constantine to St. Louis*. 2d ed. London: Longman, 1987.

Dronke, Peter. *Poetic Individuality in the Middle Ages*. Oxford: Oxford University Press, 1970.

Eynde, Damien van den. "Du nouveau sur deux maîtres lombards contemporains du Maître des Sentences." *Pier Lombardo 2* (June, 1953): 6-8.

Frugoni, Arsenio. *Arnaldo da Brescia nelle fonti del secolo xii.* Istituto Storico Italiano per il Medio Evo. Studi Storici 8-9. Rome: ISIME, 1954.

Fuhrmann, Horst. *Deutsche Geschichte im hohen Mittelalter*. Göttingen: Vandenhoeck & Ruprecht, 1978.

—. *Germany in the High Middle Ages, 1050-1200*. Trans. Timothy Reuter. Cambridge: Cambridge University Press, 1986.

Ganz, Peter. "Friedrich Barbarossa. Hof und Kultur." In Haverkamp ed., *Friedrich Barbarossa*, pp. 623-50.

Giesebrecht, Wilhelm von. *Geschichte der deutschen Kaiserzeit*. 4th ed. 5 vols. in 6. Braunschweig: C. A. Schwetschke und Sohn, 1875-81.

—. "Neue Gedichte auf Kaiser Friedrich I." In vol. 2 of *Sitzungsberichte der königlich bayerische Akademie der Wissenschaften. Historische Classe* (Dec. 6, 1874): 269-89.

—. "Sopra il Poema recentemente scoperto intorno all' Imperatore Federico I. Lettera al Prof. Ernesto Monaci in Roma." *Archivio della Società Romana di Storia Patria* 3 (1880): 49-62.

Gillingham, J. B. "Frederick Barbarossa. A Secret Revolutionary?" *English Historical Review* 86 (1971): 73-78.

—. "Why Did Rahewin Stop Writing the *Gesta Frederici?*" *English Historical Review* 83 (1968): 294-303.

Graves, Robert. *Count Belisarius.* 1938. Reprint, New York: Penguin Books, 1954.

Grebe, Werner. "Rainald von Dassel als Reichskanzler Friedrich Barbarossas (1156-1159)." *Jahrbuch des kölnischen Geschichtsvereins* 49 (1978): 49-74.

Gregorovius, Ferdinand. *History of the City of Rome in the Middle Ages.* Trans. Annie Hamilton. 8 vols in 13. London: G. Bell & Sons, 1894-1902.

Griffin, Miriam T. *Nero. The End of a Dynasty.* New Haven: Yale University Press, 1984.

Grundmann, Herbert. "Monumenta Germaniae Historica. Bericht für das Jahr 1959/60." *Deutsches Archiv für Erforschung des Mittelalters* 17 (1961): 1-8.

Gundlach, Wilhelm. *Heldenlieder der deutschen Kaiserzeit.* 3 vols. Innsbruck: Wagner, 1894-99.

Hall, J. B. "The 'Carmen de gestis Frederici imperatoris in Lombardia.'" *Studi Medievali,* ser. 3, 26 (1985): 969-76.

Hampe, Karl. *Germany under the Salian and Hohenstaufen Emperors.* Trans. R. F. Bennett. Totowa, NJ: Rowan & Littlefield, 1973.

Haskins, Charles Homer. "Moses of Bergamo." *Byzantinische Zeitschrift* 23 (1920): 133-42.

—. *The Renaissance of the Twelfth Century.* 1927. Reprint, Cambridge, MA: Harvard University Press, 1957.

Haverkamp, Alfred. *Medieval Germany 1056-1273.* Oxford: Oxford University Press, 1988.

—. Ed. *Friedrich Barbarossa. Handlungsspielräume und Wirkungsweisen des staufischen Kaisers.* Sigmaringen: Jan Thorbecke, 1992.

Hofmeister, Adolf. "Eine neue Quelle zur Geschichte Friedrich Barbarossas, *De ruina civitatis Terdonae.*" *Neues Archiv der Gesellschaft für ältere deutsche Geschichtskunde* 43 (1922): 89-157.

Holtzmann, Robert. "Das Carmen de Frederico I. imperatore aus Bergamo und die Anfänge einer staufischen Hofhistoriographie." *Neues Archiv der Gesellschaft für ältere deutsche Geschichtskunde* 44 (1922): 252-313.

Hyde, John Kenneth. *Society and Politics in Medieval Italy.* New York: St. Martin's, 1973.

Jarnut, Jorg. *Bergamo, 568-1098. Verfassung-, sozial-, und Wirthschaftsgeschichte einer lombardischen Stadt im Mittelalter.* Wiesbaden: Steiner, 1979.

—. "Gli inizi del Commune in Italia. Il caso di Bergamo." *Archivio Storico Bergamasco* 3 (1983): 201-12.

Johanek, Peter. "Kultur und Bildung im Umkreis Friedrich Barbarossas." In Haverkamp, ed. *Friedrich Barbarossa*, pp. 651-78.

Kenner, Hugh. *The Pound Era.* Berkeley and Los Angeles: University of California Press, 1971.

Koch, Gottfried. *Auf dem Wege zum Sacrum Imperium. Studien zur ideologischen Herrschaftsbegründung der deutschen Zentralgewalt im 11. und 12. Jahrhundert.* Forschungen zur mittelalterlichen Geschichte. Vol. 20. Vienna: Hermann Böhlaus, 1972.

Lammers, Walter. "Weltgeschichte und Zeitgeschichte bei Otto von Freising" In *Die Zeit der Staufer: Geschichte-Kunst-Kultur.* Vol. 5 Ed. Reiner Haussherr. Stuttgart: Würtembergisches Landesmuseum, 1977, pp. 77-90.

Langosch, Karl. *Die deutsche Literatur des lateinischen Mittelalters in ihrer geschichtlichen Entwicklung.* Berlin: W. de Gruyter, 1964.

—. *Politische Dichtung um Friedrich Barbarossa.* Berlin, 1943.

—. Review of *Carmen de gestis Frederici I. imperatoris in Lombardia,* by Irene Schmale-Ott. In *Mittellateinisches Jahrbuch* 6 (1970): 293-95.

Leyser, Karl. *Medieval Germany and its Neighbours, 900-1250.* London: Hambledon, 1982.

Manaresi, Cesare, ed. *Gli atti del comune di Milano fino all' anno MCCXVI.* Milan: Capriolo & Massimino, 1919.

Manitius, Max. *Geschichte der lateinischen Literatur des Mittelalters.* 3 vols. 1931. Reprint, Munich: C. H. Beck'sche Verlagsbuchhandlung, 1973.

Martines, Lauro. *Power and Imagination. City-States in Renaissance Italy.* New York: Vintage Books, 1980.

Mazzi, Angelo. *Note suburbane, con un' appendice sui mille homines Pergami del 1156.* Bergamo: Pagnoncelli, 1892.

Monaci, Ernesto. *L'Assedio di Milano nel MCLVIII secondo l'anonimo di Cod. Vat. Ottob. 1463.* Rome, 1886.

—. "Il Barbarossa e Arnaldo da Brescia in Roma." *Archivio della Società Romana di Storia Patria* 1 (1878): 459-65.

Monteverdi Angelo, see Francesco Novati.

Munz, Peter. *Frederick Barbarossa. A Study in Medieval Politics.* Ithaca: Cornell University Press, 1969.

Novati, Francesco. *Le Origini.* Vol. 2 of *Storia Letteraria d'Italia.* Continued and completed by Angelo Monteverdi. Milan: Vallardi, 1926.

Opll, Ferdinand. *Friedrich Barbarossa.* Darmstadt: Wissenschaftliche Buchgesellschaft, 1990.

—. *Stadt und Reich im 12. Jahrhundert (1125-1190).* Vienna: Hermann Böhlaus, 1986.

Ottmar, E. "Das Carmen de Friderico I. imperatore aus Bergamo und seine Beziehungen zu Otto-Rahewins *Gesta Friderici,* Gunthers *Ligurinus* und Burchard von Ursbergs *Chronik.*" *Neues Archiv der Gesellschaft für ältere deutsche Geschichtskunde* 46 (1926): 430-89.

Pacaut, Marcel. *Frederick Barbarossa*. Trans. A. J. Pomerans. New York: Charles Scribner, 1970.

Pagano, Antonio. *Sul Poema Gesta di Federico I in Italia*. Naples: Gennaro & Morano, 1906.

Panofsky, Erwin. *Renaissance and Renascences in Western Art*. 1960. Reprint, New York: Harper & Row, 1972.

Pesanti, Giovanni. "Il 'Pergaminus.' Prolegomeni ad una edizione critica." *Bergomum* 7 (1913): 1-22.

Pesenti, Antonio. "La Chiesa nel primo periodo di vita communale." In Antonio Rimoldi, Adriano Caprioli, and Luciano Vaccaro, eds. *Diocesi di Bergamo*. Brescia: Editrice La Scuola, 1988, pp. 61-90.

Pivec, K., and H. Heimpel. "Neue Forschungen zu Dietrich von Niem." *Nachrichten der Akademie der Wissenschaften in Göttingen. Philologisch-Historische Klasse* 4 (1951).

Popolo e stato in Italia nell'età di Federico Barbarossa. Alessandria e la Lega Lombarda. Relazioni al XXXIII congresso storico subalpino per la celebrazione dell'VIII centenario della fondazione di Alessandria, Alessandria, 1968. Turin: Società Storica Subalpina, 1970.

Pound, Ezra. "Date Line." In *Literary Essays*. Ed. T. S. Eliot. London: Faber & Faber, 1954.

Quinn, Kenneth. *Virgil's Aeneid. A Critical Description*. Ann Arbor: University of Michigan Press, 1968.

Raby, F. J. E. *A History of Secular Latin Poetry in the Middle Ages*. 2 vols. Oxford: Clarendon Press, 1934.

Rajna, Pio. "In Memoria di Ernesto Monaci." *Archivio della Società Romana di Storia Patria* 41 (1918): 307-52.

Reuter, Timothy. *Germany in the Early Middle Ages, c. 800-1056*. London: Longman, 1991.

Robertson, D. W., Jr. *A Preface to Chaucer. Studies in Medieval Perspectives*. Princeton: Princeton University Press, 1969.

Sanford, Eva Matthews. "The Twelfth Century. Renaissance or Proto-Renaissance?" *Speculum* 26 (1951): 635-42.

Scalvini, Maria Luisa. *Bergamo.* Bari: Laterza, 1987.

Schnell, Rüdiger, ed. *Die Reichsidee in der deutschen Dichtung des Mittelalters.* Wege der Forschung. Vol. 589. Darmstadt: Wissenschaftliche Buchgesellschaft, 1983.

Simonsfeld, Henry. *Jahrbücher des deutschen Reiches unter Friedrich I., 1152-1158.* 1908. Reprint, Berlin: Duncker & Humblot, 1967.

Southern, R. W. "Humanism and the School of Chartres." In *Medieval Humanism.* 1970. Reprint, Oxford: Basil Blackwell, 1984.

Stach, Walter. "Politische Dichtung im Zeitalter Friedrichs I., Der *Ligurinus* im Widerstreit mit Otto und Rahewin." *Neue Jahrbücher für deutsche Wissenschaft* 13 (1937): 385-410.

—. "Salve, mundi domine! Kommentierende Betrachtungen zum Kaiserhymnus des Archipoeta." *Berichte über die Verhandlungen der sächsischen Akademie der Wissenschaften zu Leipzig. Philologisch-Historische Klasse* 91,3 (1939): 5-58.

Sturm, Joseph. *Der Ligurinus. Ein deutsches Heldengedicht zum Lobe Kaiser Friedrich Rotbarts.* Studien und Darstellungen aus dem Gebiete der Geschichte. Vol. 8,1 and 2. Freiburg im Breisgau: Herder, 1911.

Szabo, Thomas. "Herrscherbild und Reichsgedanke. Eine Studie zur höfischen Geschichtsschreibung unter Friedrich Barbarossa." Ph.D. diss., Albert-Ludwig University at Freiburg, 1971.

Tellenbach, Gerd. *Church, State and Christian Society at the Time of the Investiture Contest.* Trans. and ed. R. F. Bennett. 1959. Reprint, New York: Harper & Row, 1970.

Testa, Giovanni B. *History of the War of Frederick I against the Communes of Lombardy.* London: Smith, Elder, 1877.

Timm, Albrecht. "Holtzmann, Robert." In vol 9 of *Neue Deutsche Biographie.* 1972.

Ullmann, Walter. "The Pontificate of Adrian IV." *The Cambridge Historical Journal* 11 (1955): 233-52.

—. *A Short History of the Papacy in the Middle Ages.* London: Methuen, 1972.

Usseglio, Leopoldo. *I Marchesi di Monferrato in Italia ed in Oriente durante i secoli xii e xiii.* Ed. Carlo Patrucco. 2 vols. XIX Congresso Storico Subalpino. Milan: Migletta, 1926.

Viscardi, Antonio. *Le Origini.* Vol. 1 of *Storia Letteraria d'Italia.* 4th ed. Milan: Vallardi, 1966.

Waley, Daniel Philip. *The Italian City Republics.* 3d ed. London: Longman, 1988.

Wenck, Karl. "Thadeus de Roma." *Neues Archiv der Gesellschaft für ältere deutsche Geschichtskunde* 9 (1884): 202.

—. "Thadeus de Roma." *Neues Archiv der Gesellschaft für ältere deutsche Geschichtskunde* 10 (1885): 170.

Zeillinger, Kurt. "Das erste roncaglische Lehensgesetz Friedrich Barbarossas. Das Scholarenprivileg *(Authentica Habita)* und Gottfried von Viterbo." *Römische Historische Mitteilungen* 26 (1984): 191-217.

DATE DUE

UPI 261-2505 G